ULTIMATE SUCCESS

Strategic Leadership Excellence

Chris Cebollero

Ultimate Success
Strategic Leadership Excellence

by Chris Cebollero

Copyright © 2017 Chris Cebollero

ISBN – 13: 978-1548646936
ISBN – 10: 1548646938

Acknowledgements

I would like to thank my editor, John Erich, for taking time in making this book a great read. He was very dedicated, professional and taught me a lot about my writing style. Cheers to you, sir.

Special thanks to my friends, family and social media network who took the time to sift through the many different book covers and settle on the winner. It was cool to share this development with you all, and I totally appreciate your help.

Maggie Morehead
Nick Nudell
Eric Graham Chase
Brian LaCroix
Becky Tyler
Billy Triplett
Jennifer Dones
Ginger Locke
Jay Cebollero
Cynthia Petronella
Jamison Hughes
Beckie Cargill
David Gelfund
Jon Dahlvig
Nancy Perry
Kaye Sheets
Josephine Lume
Karole Sorge-Dubowsky
Josh Ishmael
Debbie Self
Patty Moakley
Stephanie Conway
Tricia O'Laughlin
Jennifer Cordia
Maddi Cordia
Kennedy Cordia

Lisa Vollrath
Holly Stewart
Daud Husami
Lisa Richard
Kendric Lynn
Ryan Greenberg
Matt Guy
Rommie Duckworth
Cheryl Willis
April McKenzie
Patricia Patterson
Donna Alessi
Jon Puryear
Dave Miles
Ruben Farnsworth
Rebecca Poindexter
Caden Carr
Mark Hammond
Laura Denton
Janet Schulte
Kathy Summers
Corinne Bottoni
Charlene Barber
Becky Porter
Kristin Soares
Lauren Porter

William McKenna
Jen Royer
Bec O'Bar
Jimmy Stix
Chris Giusto
Connie Meyer
Kenneth McKenzie
Kimberly Shrewsberry
Andy Keeven
Tracey Loscar
JoAnne Bandiero
Michael Cline
Kara Marquez
Jeff Ellison
Ian Breden
Catie Holstein
Melissa Werlinger
Monica Emde
Becky Tyler
Rick Bazan
Bradley Dean
Shane Parker
Dave Nestor
Lisa Bureau
Jaye Gustafson
Tim Gash

Isabelle Cordia
Charlene Baker
Jamie Davis
Stephanie Limmer
Dave Konig
Rose Jordan
Joyce Brown
Tony O'Brien
Dave Aber
John Broyles
Rhonda Pogue Smiley
Margaret Keavney
Roger Smith

Lee Cebollero
Angela Cebollero
Zachery Cebollero
TC Bradley
Darla Kemp
Macara Trusty
Leslie Williams
Jamie Lee Wright
Debbie Knight
KC Jones
Chris & Renee Bryant
Gregg Luedtke
Jayme Miles

Nena Lee
Liz Roberts
Andrea Stevens

This book is dedicated to my beautiful, smart and funny grandbabies. You all bring a smile to my face and warm my heart, especially when I get to watch you make your parents frustrated, crazy and want to pull their hair out. Poppa loves you all.

Reilley Austin
Alexander Ryan
Adalynn Marie
Hudson James
Brooklyn Grace

Advance Praise

"In *Ultimate Success,* Chris Cebollero presents practical, wise, specific advice to help any leader to be more effective. He distills personal, hard-earned lessons into solid guidance for the rest of us. The book is addressed to new leaders, but it seems relevant for those with experience as well. I know I'll be referring to this text for years to come."

—Charles A. "Chad" Weinstein, PhD,
***Author of* Thinking Aloud: Reflections on Ethical Leadership**

"Chris Cebollero once again outlines the tools leaders need to complete their 'Ultimate' journey. You can feel the wisdom, understand the strategy and develop the plan that will assist you in achieving your success as a leader. There are many points for reflection that allow the reader to apply the suggested strategy. This is a reference that you can and will use for years to come."

—Maureen Metcalf,
***Author of* Innovative Leadership Fieldbook**

"Chris's book and experience confirm the fact that everyone has the potential to be a leader. No one is born with leadership abilities; it is something that is developed throughout the years and worked on daily. This book helps you find out who you are, the environment you can thrive in, and how you can use that ability to serve others."

—Anna Sarnacka–Smith,
***Author of* Everest Lidera**
Soon to be translated into English

Contents

Introduction

Welcome to my second book in the Ultimate Leadership development series. In my first installment, *Ultimate Leadership: 10 Rules for Success,* I outlined the rules I had to come up with to be the best leader possible. Those rules developed from my successes, failures and lessons learned over my 30-year career. This installment, *Ultimate Success: Strategic Leadership Excellence,* will outline the skills that will assist you in developing your leadership style into one that ensures leadership excellence.

You may have heard it before: Leadership is both an art and a science. It is vital you understand the science before you can paint a picture of individual and organizational success. In this reference we will discuss the elements of developing "ultimate success."

It's your job as a leader to get the very best out of your workforce. They are your most precious resource, and often your most neglected. How do organizations grow? It should start with a vision statement, setting goals to reach that vision, then developing plans to reach those goals. Honestly, that is the easy part of organizational success. Next you'll need to engage the workforce toward implementing the plans to reach the goals that make the vision a reality. Not many leaders even understand that concept, much less understand the science of developing a successful organization or workforce.

As I engage with organizations to craft the best plan for their development, one of the commonalities in most organizations is the mentality of company leaders who do not regard the workforce as their responsibility.

Your focus as a leader is to make certain your workforce is your most important duty and responsibility. Be careful of the corporate mind-set; you will be overworked doing budgets, creating schedules, and in countless meetings and projects that take time away from that most precious resource. With all that BS of responsibility, the area that needs your constant focus is neglected. Your workforce is the defining measure of your success. Concentrate on creating a culture that will grow, polish and move them to the next level of their success. As your workforce watches you focus your efforts on them, as they learn to trust you and come to you with suggestions and comments, you will watch their satisfaction and engagement mature. Once this begins to happen, you will become a go-to leader, and then you will develop your credibility and reputation and gain ultimate success.

In this book you will find the blueprint to become a leader that will allow the workforce to see just how crucial they are to organizational success. Learn and adapt these skills, and you will achieve leadership excellence.

Thank you once again for allowing me to join you on your professional development journey. I appreciate you and look forward to hearing your comments and suggestions.

CHAPTER ONE
Your Leadership Definition

"The quality of a leader is reflected in the standards they set for themselves."

—Ray Kroc

DEFINING LEADERSHIP

The first step in developing into a great leader must start with understanding what exactly leadership is, what it means to you and how you can apply it toward developing into a great leader. Though this sounds like a simple step, it is one that is often overlooked. It is vital for your success as a leader to understand these three questions and make them the foundation of your leadership.

1. **What is leadership?** Very simply, leadership is a verb, not a noun. It is not your title or accomplishments or even your ability to manage. Leadership is an action you display every day. Since we are on the topic of defining leadership, believe it or not, in today's workforce there is still confusion between leadership and management. There shouldn't be. You manage processes, schedules and budgets; you lead people. We will get more into the process of leading people in the next section as we discuss putting your leadership knowledge into practice.

2. **What does leadership mean to you?** When you look up leadership online, you will find countless definitions. Clients often ask me the "true" definition of leadership. My answer is very simply this: "What does leadership mean to you?" This is

your foundation, your belief, your teaching. Maybe it is not right according to the book definition, or it may need some polishing or refinement, but it is your place to begin your leadership journey. By the time you've gotten well into that journey, your definition may have grown or morphed into something totally different than it is today. Regardless, the journey begins with your definition. I encourage you to give yourself a minute to define your concept of leadership. As we continue together, let's see how that definition develops.

3. **How can you apply your definition into becoming a great leader?** Think about the best leaders you've ever worked with. What characteristics did they have? What attributes did you want to emulate? What made them worthy of your consideration as a great leader? Now let's flip the coin and ask about the worst boss you ever worked for. What were those horrible characteristics they displayed that made you want to take out your own gallbladder with a spoon rather than go into work? What characteristics did they have? What attributes did you swear you'd never emulate if you were a boss? These are important lessons in starting off as a leader.

Answering the above questions will assist in outlining your leadership vision. Now let's do another assignment: Define your concept of leadership, and outline the characteristics you want to display as a leader and how you want to apply these attributes to your leadership style. Let's call this your personal leadership vision statement.

When you think about the best leader you've ever worked for, think about the characteristics they had that made you respect and want to follow them. These are important parts of your leadership development; these traits and lessons from past leaders assist in shaping the leaders we'll eventually become.

I say *eventually* because we still want to test the water with our own knowledge, skills and experience. It is not until our thinking starts to go south that we then think about how to redefine our leadership style.

My first lesson in leadership came as a member of the United States Air Force. As an impressionable 19-year-old, I was molded, guided and conditioned into becoming the best *airman* possible. There was yelling and finger-pointing but not much guidance or coaching. So as I developed, my leadership style grew from what I was accustomed to. As a young leader, I had no interest in what my troops thought, needed or wanted from a leader. Of course it goes without saying that I was not very effective as a leader in my first decade.

Now, the lesson here was not only that I was ineffective as a leader, but for the next 10 years my incompetence grew, my empathy was nonexistent and my ability to coach failed miserably. But in the Air Force, my troops had no recourse to complain. This was the standard— this was how most us acted.

Once I left the military and entered the dreaded world of the private sector, my arrogance, ego and poor leadership skills followed me. Again for the *next* 10 years (that would be 20 now, if you're keeping count), I failed as a leader and had to learn the proper way to lead and grow a productive workforce.

GETTING THE BEST OUT OF PEOPLE

The primary role of a leader is to motivate, inspire and get the very best out of those in their charge. Organizations need a strong, engaged, satisfied and productive force to build to the next level of success. This is where your leadership skills become invaluable to the organizations that hire you for your expertise.

When you hold a position responsible for leadership of others, you must remember you're engaged in a team sport. You are the captain of a team, and you're responsible for guiding it to a championship. No one person brings a team to greatness; it takes an all-hands-on-deck approach. When I engage with organizations, it is surprising to see how many individuals in leadership positions do not have this mentality. They will say things like, "They should be happy they have jobs," "Why should I thank them? They receive a paycheck every two weeks," and "They need to do what I tell them to do." It's no wonder these organizations are engaging with a leadership consultant!

One of the most common questions I ask is, "Would you work for you?" If they say yes, that's a different issue. Here is a secret (come closer to the book): The days of command and control, or leading from a position of authority, are over. Today leaders need to start with a foundation of service.

What is the best way to develop your workforce, motivate them, inspire them and assist them in doing the best job possible? This is the big question. The best answer is to give them what they will need to be successful. That thing is *you*. You have to be the force that guides them, grows them and assists them to achieving greatness.

Robert Greenleaf outlined "servant leadership" in the mid-1970s. Servant leadership consists of 10 elements: listening, empathy, healing, awareness, persuasion, conceptualization, foresight, stewardship, commitment to the growth of people, and building community. While there are many leadership styles, the successful leader must use a palette of strategies to lead many types of personalities, but at your base servant leadership will give you the footing to become successful.

There are certainly many traditional leadership styles out there, and a good leader uses a combination of them. As a leader you will not lead all individuals the same way. How you lead an entry-level employee is different than how you lead a veteran. Therefore, knowing the traditional leadership styles come in handy. But regardless of what leadership style you're working with, you need to keep servant leadership as your foundational method of guiding your workforce.

A solid leadership style is just half the equation. The other half that leads to success is the attributes that influence people to follow you. While there are countless attributes, it is paramount that you develop the qualities that will inspire, motivate and guide your workforce to success. Leadership attributes are developed based on personality, self-confidence and the values of the individual leader. The characteristics I have as a leader may be totally different than the ones in your toolbox. We can be equally successful with different characteristics in accomplishing the mission.

There are some common qualities leaders should display. These include:

1. **Vision**—Being able to portray what future success looks like to your workforce is a must for success.

> ### *Vision Statement*
>
> The vision statement is one of the most important components of an organization's success. When speaking to leaders, I love to ask, "How many of your organizations have a vision statement?" You can see the hands go up with pride. The next question shuts this down quickly: "Who can *come up here and recite it for me?*" If you as the leader do not know what the vision statement is, how can the workforce assist the organization in becoming successful?

2. **Decisiveness**—Decisions need to be made, and as the leader you must make them. Decisiveness comes down to more than just making a timely choice; it includes fostering confidence, including others, choosing the best answer for the moment, then putting that plan into action. Sometimes decisions may fail, and that's OK. Share the mistake, discuss the lesson learned and move on. You will be seen as a leader of action instead of one paralyzed by indecision.

3. **Positive attitude**—Having a positive attitude, being optimistic and showing passion is such an important leadership trait that it gets its own chapter. We will examine it more in Chapter Two.

4. **Accountability**—This is a vital component to becoming a successful leader. Being accountable means not just savoring the glory of good achievements, but taking more than your share of the blame when things don't work out. I've engaged with countless leaders who were professionals in passing blame. They'd point fingers at others; poor results never had to do with their leadership or guidance (when in fact it all had to do with their poor leadership). "But, Chris, that problem was out of my control!" Well, my friend, when you are a leader, everything you manage or lead should be in your control. When

you blame others, you're a victim, and when you play victim, you're not a leader. Great leaders will take the reins, show the way, initiate influence and take responsibility for the results.

5. **Courage**—Sometimes the decisions a leader makes will not be popular, and making them may cause "a great disturbance in the force." This is where you must be brave and confident.

Courage

During the crisis in Ferguson, Mo., in 2014, my No. 1 concern was ensuring my crews made it home at the ends of their shifts. The thought of having to share with a family that their loved one was hurt or worse was not something I wanted to do. Some areas of Ferguson and the surrounding cities were violent and deemed "hot" zones.

At one point there were not enough police units available, with everything else going on, for our ambulances to receive police escort into those hot zones. I decided that in the absence of force protection (no police escort), the ambulances would not respond to any 9-1-1 calls.

The first time this occurred a patient had to walk through some woods to get to a waiting ambulance. The paramedic in charge of the call contacted me after the call was completed. Let's just say they were very emotional and speaking with great conviction. Finally they asked me how could I make such a horrible decision. My response was very clear and calm: "I made that decision so when you get off work, you will go home to your wife and daughter." In the end he understood my decision and applauded my courage.

---

6. **Self-motivation**—This is one of the most important and toughest qualities for a leader. It is the motivated leader who has a desire to achieve the greatest vision; your motivation stokes the fire of your internal passion, pride and desire to become the best you can. It is this fire that others will find

contagious and want to emulate, and it will stoke their motivation in turn.

"People often say that motivation doesn't last. Well, neither does bathing—that's why we recommend it daily."

—Zig Ziglar

7. **Charisma**—One of the components of being a leader is that you need to have followers. One of the very first qualities individuals will see is you. My friend and mentor John Maxwell says, "People buy into the leader before they buy into the vision. This is where your personality should shine, your message be clear, your philosophy showcased." Not all leaders have this trait, and even though they are great leaders, it takes them longer to convince those around them.

Charisma

Early in my career I began working for a leader who always seemed like he was about to commit a double homicide. It constantly looked like he was trying to decide where to hide the bodies. When I asked a coworker about him, my colleague was quick to tell me that talking to this boss was like watching paint dry. He had a dry sense of humor; when he spoke he was deliberate and brief. I thought he was going to be a difficult man to work for.

As time passed and he made his vision known and displayed his caring and ability to make decisions, I began to respect his approach. I remember being amazed that he seemed to have an answer to every challenge, and the answer always came with an explanation of how he learned to choose it.

This man I thought would be difficult to work for actually became one of the best leaders I've met in my professional career. With all things similar, though, if he'd been more blessed with charisma, I would have gotten there a lot sooner.

8. **Ethics**—One of the best pieces of advice I can share here is to know and understand your own values and beliefs. Once you do that, being an ethical leader means never compromising those beliefs or values. Use this as a blueprint to develop a moral code within your team and guide how it approaches things. You will find your standard sets the stage for your staff's decisions and behaviors. Depending on your stage of leadership, you will face pressures to compromise your beliefs, and you will make the best decisions in those situations. Here's some hindsight from my experiences: When you are not true to yourself, you cannot be true to others.

9. **Loyalty**—This is an attribute that is critical for leadership success. Being loyal to your organization, workforce, peers and career field is essential when you are guiding others. If you do not display the trait of loyalty, no one else will either.

10. **Emotional intelligence**—Leading with emotional intelligence is one of those attributes all leaders need and few possess. In my book *Ultimate Leadership: 10 Rules for Success,* rule No. 1 is to never allow your emotions to dictate your actions. How many times have you seen leaders react emotionally, and it negatively affects their credibility? It is essential for maintaining your credibility to keep a level head and control your emotions.

Begin your growth as a successful leader with your personal definition of leadership. From there polish it, cultivate it and continue to redefine it. You will see great things happen as your understanding of the meaning of leadership grows.

CHAPTER TWO

You Are the Difference Maker

"Attitude is a little thing that makes a big difference."

—Winston Churchill

I will tell you from the very beginning: This is the most important chapter for your continued success. People are always looking for that secret ingredient that will help them become successful, but they never seem to find it. Well, here it is: Your success as a leader rises and falls on what you think, how you feel and the behaviors those feelings create. Basically your attitude sets the stage for your successes and failures. It is your positive behavior that is the difference maker. There is a great quote by football coach Lou Holtz that says, "Ability is what you are capable of doing, motivation determines what you do, attitude determines how well you do it." Your ability and motivation matter, but it's the attitude you have while doing what you do that makes the difference.

This is going to be one of those chapters you must become friends with, study, understand and continually reread throughout your career.

When I was younger people would say to me, "You have a bad attitude," or "Has anyone ever told you have an attitude problem?" At the time maybe that was true, but those individuals pointing the finger at me were likely the reason I had that attitude! How many poor attitudes come from poor leadership? How much of your negative attitude developed because your company did not know how to treat people? This one is my favorite: How did it affect your attitude when you were the victim of favoritism or a double standard?

As we discuss exactly what an attitude is and the things that influence your attitudes, consider this: If you, as a leader, took the time to figure out the catalysts for negative or bad behaviors, you could develop solutions to address them. But before we talk more about this, let's do some education on attitude.

ATTITUDE DEFINED

When you try to define attitude, what comes to mind? The dictionary defines attitude as *a settled way of thinking or feeling about someone or something, typically one that is reflected in a person's behavior.* So, it should go not only with how you feel but also how you show that feeling outwardly.

WHAT INFLUENCES ATTITUDES?

There are several factors that sway attitude, and how we choose to react to these influencers can be positive or negative. Here are a few of the influencers that affect our attitudes.

Whom we are as people—This goes to the foundation of who you are as a person. We can add the discussion of nature vs. nurture, how your personality developed and how you choose to carry yourself. In 1984 I joined the U.S. Air Force. My love of country grew from my many years as a member of this brotherhood. My attitude toward the United States was forged by my service, loyalty and swearing to protect her from enemies. It was this foundation of attitude that still carries me today.

What is happening around us—It makes no difference if it's something big or small. I remember growing up in New York City. For a kid of Italian ancestry, the food was always awesome and plentiful. One week my mother said she would make baked ziti on Sunday. Anticipating this delicious gift of tastes propelled me through the week. When Sunday came my mother got carried away during a lengthy phone call and burned the ziti. I remember realizing, at 12 years old, that I was not going to enjoy my beloved baked ziti. I was mad, disappointed and hurt. Let's just say my attitude was not one of a respectful young man, and I had some very nasty comments ready to come out. Ultimately those comments stayed internal—far be it for me to have an attitude problem with my mother. She would have very graciously stabbed me in the eye with a fork if I'd been disrespectful about the ziti. But you get the point: What happens around us affects our attitude.

Your feelings—These are a big influence on attitude. Sometimes our attitude is unwarranted as we fight through feelings. Here is what happens: We have thoughts; those thoughts create feelings; those feelings then create behaviors. What those thoughts and feelings are will result in either a positive or negative attitude. Spending the time to reflect and understand those feelings will assist in developing the self-awareness necessary to eventually get to a state of leading with emotional intelligence.

Your experiences—Can you think about a time where your experience influenced your attitude? Was it on a vacation? A discussion with your boss? Maybe a spat with your spouse? I can tell you with certainty, fighting with your spouse or significant other can impact your attitude.

Your relationships—Have you ever had a negative attitude because of someone you knew? That one person at work who, when you saw them coming, you just knew you were going to have an attitude with them? Often there's one person who pushes your buttons and whom you'd rather jump out a window than deal with. Well, regardless of the person, relationships affect us all positively and negatively.

What you believe—Our belief systems affect us in many ways. During the 2016 presidential election, conflicts abounded among friends with different beliefs. You'd make one small comment about your candidate, and it was like being thrown to the lions in the Roman Colosseum. But we developed attitudes based on our beliefs.

How you see yourself—Your self-esteem and self-confidence play a huge factor in developing your attitude. Again, this can be both positive and negative. How you see yourself is an important factor in the success of not only whom you are but, more important, whom you want to become.

There are many factors that influence your attitude, and one of the important ones here is that you get to be the one who determines how these influencers impact you. Regardless of the influence, you get to choose how you react to your experiences, beliefs and relationships.

You and only you are the sole control over how you think, feel and react.

An Attitude for Success

Throughout the day there can be several things that pop up and affect us, guiding our attitude one way or another. You could be in a good mood and then spill coffee on your desk; you could be in a foul mood and then speak to someone on the phone who lifts your spirits. You and only you have the power over your attitude. The realization is this: No one can make you feel anything you choose not to feel.

I'm sure you have heard someone say, "They hurt my feelings." Well, whatever was said to you, you *allowed* that to hurt your feelings. Once you understand that no one can make you feel anything you choose not to feel, you will not only feel happier but will also save mega dollars on psychiatric fees.

Controlling Your Attitude

Your thoughts create feelings, your feelings create behaviors, your behaviors create more thoughts and feelings. It is a terrible circle, and if you don't get a handle on it, it'll have you running in circles for years and years. One of the questions I get most often when coaching clients is how to control the negative self-talk we endure in our heads.

What Is Self-Talk?

You know that voice, the one that sits in our heads. It shares its opinion, helps us make sense of situations, passes judgment on others. Oh, yeah, that voice. Our inner voice is our self-talk. It develops with the assistance of our conscious mind, beliefs, external influences, experiences and (the biggest culprit of all) the subconscious mind. Since this book is about secrets to ultimate success, here is another one: That self-talk sometimes is not the friend we make it out to be. It can be rebellious, harmful, sabotage success and wound self-esteem and self-confidence. Just between you and me, if I knew where that little voice lived, I'd perform a drive-by.

TYPES OF SELF-TALK

For years there was this voice in my head—let's call him Dennis. It seemed Dennis always had something to say. I'd say, "I'm going to the gym," Dennis would say, "Take a nap instead." If I needed to study for a test, Dennis would want to go hang out with girls. (Honestly, I didn't mind Dennis's guidance in that area.) Dennis always had a way of making things easy.

During my school years, my goal was to become part of the high school baseball team. Before tryouts you had to attend an orientation that outlined expectations, rules and such. I remember wanting so badly to get on this team. But as I looked around the room, there were guys there I thought were bigger than me, faster, maybe better with the bat.

As I prepared my equipment for the next day's tryout, Dennis was there to give me his advice: *I know you want on this team, but what really makes you think you can be successful? You know you must practice after school every day. You really think you're better than all those bigger guys you saw today?* Well, Dennis made a lot of sense, and so I skipped the tryouts and went home instead. That night was full of disappointment, and even though Dennis was happy, I felt miserable. That night dinner sucked, TV sucked, conversation was boring. But it was the next day that made that spring and summer suck the most: As I walked through the halls at school, the baseball coach pulled me aside and asked why I missed tryouts. My response was something rebellious, I'm sure. His next words still cut deeply today: "I was truly looking forward to your glove at second base this year." He walked away, and I felt like a failure.

Everyone battles with their negative self-talk. It causes you to change your mind, reminds you how apprehensive you are, keeps you from following your dreams, keeps you inside your comfort zone and deters you from working hard. Remember when I said if I knew where Dennis lived, I would perform a drive-by? Well, I know his exact location, and this holds true for your inner voice as well: Your inner voice is a resident of your subconscious mind.

TRAINING YOUR SUBCONSCIOUS MIND

It is a great honor for me to call John Maxwell a friend and mentor. One of the benefits of being a member of the John Maxwell team is being mentored by John and his teaching team. One lesson I want to share with you comes from Christian Simpson. Christian is a globally recognized coach to the coaches.

Thurman Fleet, DC, was a chiropractor in Texas in the first half of the 20th century. Dr. Fleet became worried that he was not making his patients well and began looking for evidence his patients' problems were more psychological than physical.

His response to this was to develop what he termed *concept therapy,* or *conceptology, this is also a big component of Cognitive Behavior Therapy.* What Dr. Fleet wanted to do was give his patients a visual idea of how they could assist in their own healing. Accordingly he developed the stick person we will discuss below. If we think about your mind, we can say there is a conscious mind and a subconscious mind.

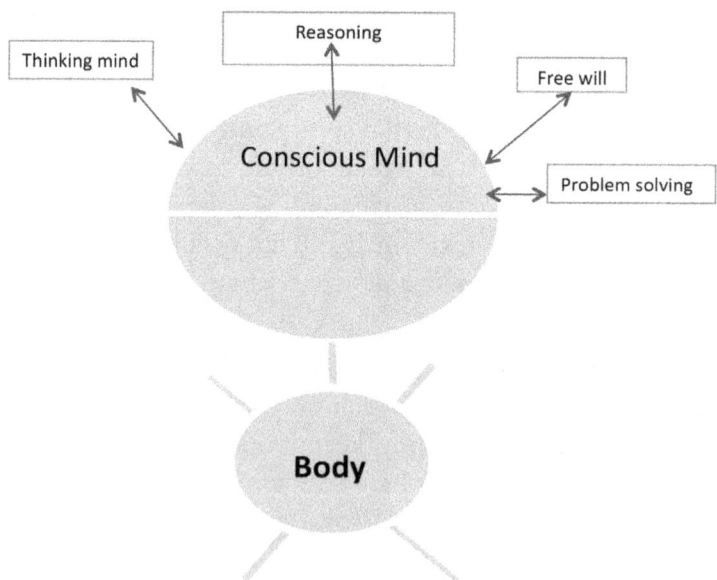

Figure 1—Your conscious mind is your thinking mind. This is where your IQ is housed, your reasoning, problem solving and critical thinking. This is also where your current level of awareness lives.

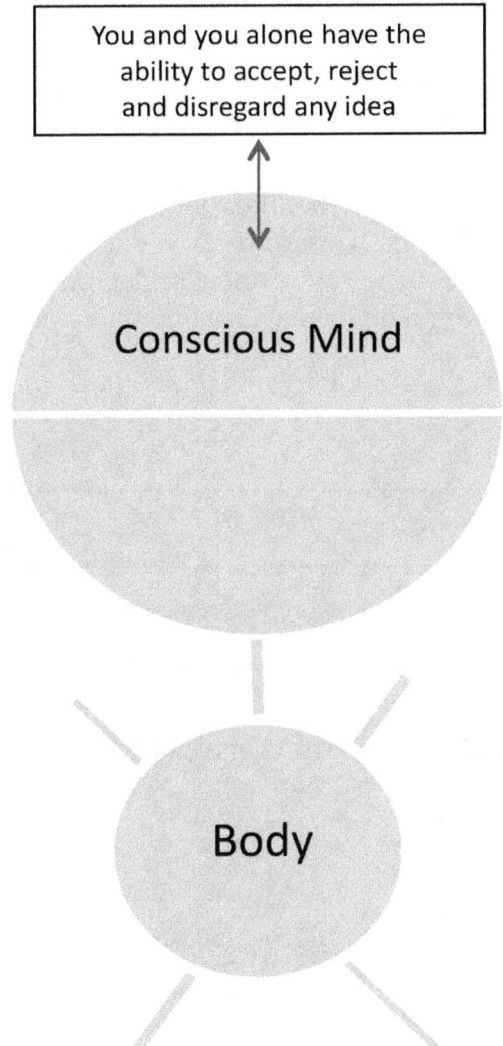

Figure 2—Within your conscious mind you also have the ability accept, reject or disregard any idea. It does not matter if this idea comes from your own imagination or external sources. Your free will, reasoning and ability to think allow you to choose what to believe. If someone shares an idea that the sky is green, you know without a doubt this is false, and you choose not to believe it. On the other hand, if the argument is good enough, you may consider that in fact the sky may be green. This is your choice, and you have this ability.

Now, there is a very important concept here that should be understood: Knowing that you can accept, reject or disregard any idea, it's you and you alone who is responsible for what you believe, and you can never blame anyone else because you weighed the data and made the choice. Your choice is a function of your awareness, and no one else can make that choice for you.

The conscious mind also has the ability to form ideas for change, growth and improvement. Unfortunately it does not have the responsibility or power to make any of these achievements a reality. That responsibility falls on the subconscious mind.

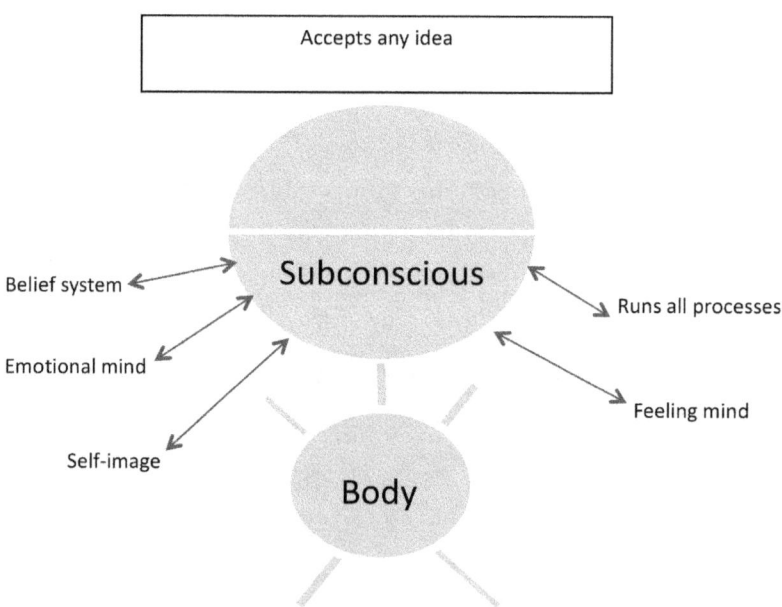

Figure 3—Your subconscious mind is where your emotional intelligence (EQ) resides. Your EQ has power and influence over your IQ. Think about that for a second: You may have great intelligence, but it is your EQ that takes control of situations. As you develop as a leader, it is vital that you combine your IQ and EQ and lead equally with your smarts and feelings.

Other functions of the subconscious mind include your belief system, self-esteem and spirituality. One of its most important components remains the ability to control all the body's systems and processes. Every body system, organ and cell is controlled by the subconscious mind, and it occurs automatically.

Now, what we will discuss here is the key to your ultimate success. Once you understand this concept, there will be nothing that stands in the way of achieving your personal or professional success.

Unlike the conscious mind, which can accept, reject or disregard an idea, the subconscious mind can only *accept ideas.* Think about this concept for a moment: Whatever idea you accept—"I'm never going to quit smoking!" "I'm never going to lose weight!" "I'm a failure!"— your subconscious mind will believe it as truth.

As you continually repeat and believe these statements, they become engraved on your subconscious mind. This impression will eventually become second nature and instill behaviors or habits that further make these truths a reality. Remember, your subconscious mind controls the body and creates habits that make processes easier for us.

We started down this rabbit hole by discussing the power of negative self-talk. Let's look at an example of wanting to diet. You put a diet and exercise plan in place (step #1). As the diet continues, it becomes harder to change habits, and you say to yourself, "I am never going to lose weight!" (#2). Since your subconscious mind can only accept the ideas you give it, it believes you are never going to lose weight (#3). Since your subconscious mind believes you will never lose weight, it causes your body to act to support this truth (#4).

Putting it all together, you say to yourself you are never going to lose weight, then your subconscious mind believes it to be true, your subconscious mind puts your body in action to support the belief you will never lose weight, and you eat pie. Once you eat the pie, you feel horrible, you tell yourself you will never lose weight, and the cycle continues.

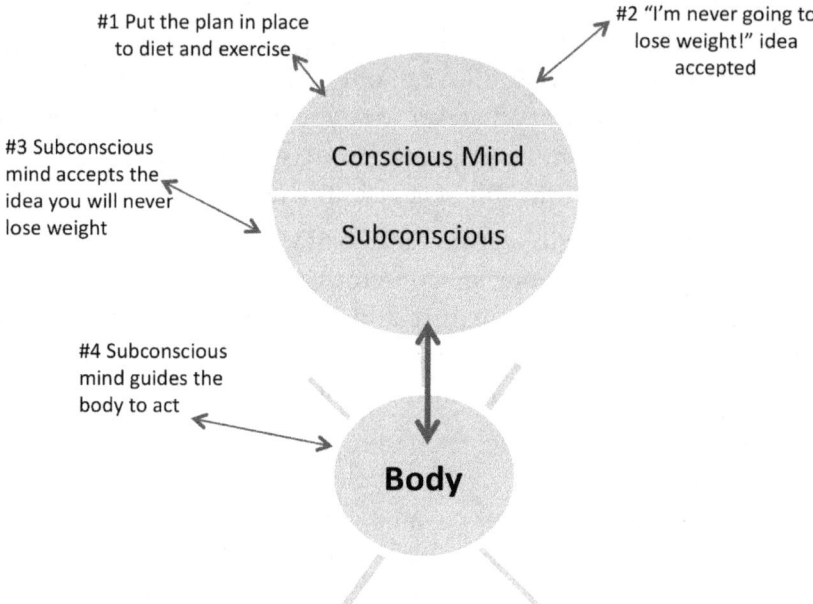

Figure 4—The intention is good. Maybe your clothes aren't fitting well or you're getting ready for swimsuit weather. In your conscious mind, you discuss all the things you need to do to begin and set a plan.

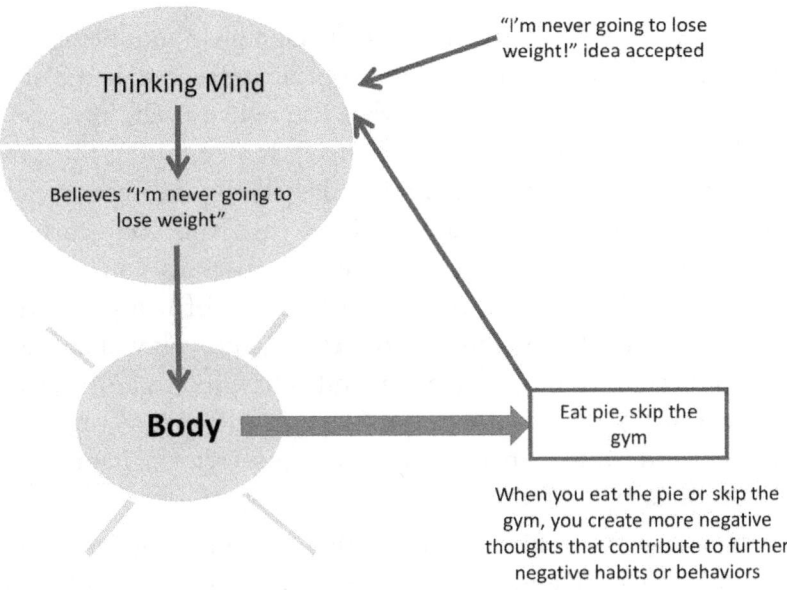

Figure 5—So the fateful day comes, and you begin cutting out sugar, eliminating caffeine and reducing carbs. You make it to the gym several days in a row. You now begin to feel tired, sore and aren't eating as many calories. Now comes the negative self-talk: "This is hard," "I'm never going to lose weight," "I'm just going to be fat." As you have these ideas, your subconscious mind believes them as truths and operates for you the one thing it controls: your body. When you walk past the pie, your subconscious mind tells you "You're never going to lose weight, have a piece of pie! You're never going to lose weight, let's skip the gym and sleep later!"

Your subconscious mind does not know it is hurting you; it is only doing what you are telling it to do.

"I am never going to lose weight."

"I am never going to quit smoking."

"I am a failure."

THE POWER OF POSITIVE

There's tons of talk up in the past paragraphs about being negative, but all is not lost. The true secret to ultimate success is the ability to change the way you see things, what you tell yourself, how you think and how you see yourself. Your first step in developing this powerful ally is to change the way you think and challenge the negative self-talk. You must remember, the die has been cast, and your current level of awareness is being driven by the subconscious you've developed for yourself. As you continue down the path of being negative, the power of your subconscious mind kicks in, and you will continue the cycle of negative thoughts, feelings and behaviors. You must, from this day forward, focus on the power of positive in every aspect of your personal and professional life. This is your secret to a happier life and professional success.

Just as with working out or dieting, as you set out to change the way you think, "Dennis" is going to be there to tell you how stupid you are and unsuccessful you'll be. Without self-control, focus and self-awareness, you will continue to fall victim.

CHALLENGING THE STATUS QUO

Believe me, team, once you begin this journey, you will begin to feel better about your work and achievements—and, more important, about yourself as a person and professional. Stop doubting yourself. Motivational speaker Les Brown says, "There is greatness within you," and he is 100% correct. You must believe in yourself and compete to win. Why did other people deserve to be on the high school baseball team and I didn't? Because they believed in themselves, and I didn't. Who are other people to tell you are not good enough? Prove them wrong.

Challenge negative self-talk. It is easy to assume your thoughts are facts. You set the "truths" within your subconscious, and you should be the one to establish more positive truths. Perceptions are not truth; what other people think about you is not truth. Past failures do not define your future successes. You have to break this cycle, and only you can do it.

When negative thoughts pop into your head, challenge them with these tips:

1. **Self-awareness**—The first thing you need to do is recognize this is happening. Once these behaviors become habits, you may not even know they're occurring anymore. Remember, your subconscious mind creates behaviors and eventually habits based on your thoughts. There may be behaviors you're not even noticing you're doing.

2. **Supporting documentation**—This is the reality test that confronts those thoughts. Ask yourself what evidence supports your thinking. Determine if thoughts are based on perception or facts.

3. **Alternative reasons**—Determine whether there's a different way to look at the issue. Think, *what else could this mean?* If you were to think positively, how would it change the situation?

4. **Put it into perspective**—It's all about the perspective and weight you place on the situation. Is it a bad situation, or am I making it into a bad situation? What is the best that can happen? Is there anything good about this situation? Will it matter in a year?

5. **Find the opportunity**—If you feel something is a problem, find the opportunity in it. How can you come out on the other side with a win? Change your focus to determining how to achieve goals, fix problems and learn something.

6. **Your vision statement**—So you need to reprogram your subconscious to be more positive. Write yourself a personal vision statement and read it several times a day until you see a change in your behavior.

To conclude this chapter, let's return to the big truth: You and you alone control your thoughts, feelings, behavior and success. It is paramount to your ultimate success to think and be positive. There is a great quote to close this chapter, usually attributed to the late businessman Frank Outlaw:

"Watch your thoughts, they become words.

Watch your words, they become actions.

Watch your actions, they become habits.

Watch your habits, they become your character.

Watch your character, it becomes your destiny."

CHAPTER THREE

It All Comes Back to Communication

"The art of communication is the language of leadership."

—James Humes

For a leader, communication is the foundation of success. When we think about the topic of communication, we can outline some direct and concrete guidelines. In this chapter we are going to focus on the importance of communication, its components and its practices. This will allow you to get a foothold as you prepare to determine how to take your communication skills to the next level.

In 2014 Ferguson, Mo., was thrust into the international spotlight when a white police officer shot an African-American teen. This was the catalyst for 19 days of civil unrest. This was a very emotional time for my workforce and organization, not to mention our community. Our operational challenges included an absence of unified command, poor communication and misinformation.

The information I needed as chief of an emergency medical services department was vital to make certain ambulances were placed in the proper position to optimize response and patient care. Unfortunately, none of the needed information was funneling down to the folks doing the work. As my leadership team and I scrambled to do the best we could with minimal information, we had little to share with the workforce.

This was a trying time. Rioting, looting and assaults were occurring every day. Ambulances were hit with rocks and bottles; some fire stations were fired upon. Occupants of another car brandished a gun at an ambulance crew stopped at a red light. Personnel were concerned for their personal safety and needed to know what the organization's leaders knew. Workers who weren't receiving information from their leaders, from those in charge, felt lost and left out.

The true communication breakdown here came from me not sharing with that there was nothing new to share. They assumed we were keeping vital strategies, plans and information from them. As this frustration boiled, I had to realize my mistake: In the absence of communication and information, there will grow frustration, fear and the creation of people's own stories and scenarios. What was more vital, I realized that when the communication stops, the fighting starts.

This was a very important lesson for me: that even in the absence of information, communication is still the foundation of organizational success.

Below are some practical techniques and tips to help organize your thoughts and consider communication somewhat systematically while looking at the communication process itself.

The Communication Process

There are four main components needed for effective communication:

1. A communicator (a person with something to say),

2. A message (what the communicator wishes to say),

3. A receiver (the person to whom the message is directed), and

4. Feedback (confirmation that the message was received and understood correctly)

In some ways the last of these, feedback, is the most important. Most immediately feedback informs the communicator whether the message was received as intended. Further, we all need feedback to develop our communication skills over time.

Sometimes when we miscommunicate it is only because we forget about one or more of these components. Sometimes we don't spend the time we need on the message before we start "transmitting." Think about how hard it can be to listen to someone "think out loud."

Other times we are so focused on our message that we neglect the perspective of the receiver. Are they in a position to hear and consider our message? Many communication problems can be solved just by focusing on these basics.

There are many other things that can go wrong in the communication process as well. First, as the communicator, you should think about how your specific message should be delivered. Sharing a message filled with jargon and business terms with a peer may be different than sharing the same message with a layperson. Deciding how to frame a message is known as *encoding*. The message is delivered to the receiver and must be unpackaged to determine what it means. This is known as *decoding*. We have all been in a situation where we said something and the person we were taking to decoded a different message than we meant. This was a breakdown in the process, leading to miscommunication.

For successful communication to transpire, you as the leader must take the time necessary to become an expert communicator. Here are some of the skills you need to add to your leadership toolbox for successful communication.

Listen to grow—There is a great quote I love from the Dalai Lama: "When you talk you are only repeating what you already know, but when you listen you may learn something new." As a leader it is vital for your ultimate success to learn something new every chance you get.

Most leaders I meet in coaching sessions listen to answer rather than listen to understand. People often develop their response before the communicator has completed their entire message. This is such a failure on the part of the listener; you could be forming a response to a concern or question that may never come! I cannot count the number of times when, acting as a mediator, someone lays out a problem, and the listener responds, and the person communicating says, "What does that have to do with what I just said?" The person listening just shut down to work on their response instead of listening to the entire message. Sometimes, with some prodding and direct questions, you may be able to guide the communicator to finding the answers themselves.

What is the best way to listen? Ensure you have an open mind, listen to the message and decode it appropriately. To do this you must listen to how the message is delivered. The goal is to actively listen to and concentrate on the speaker. You must ignore distractions and deadlines and minimize interruptions. Allow the communicator to talk, avoid interrupting, make eye contact, smile, nod and use proper questioning techniques to clarify and reflect on the message and give appropriate feedback.

For years leaders have been told that they need to listen to their employees: "Your success depends on listening to what your employees say." Well, prepare yourself for this nugget of wisdom: Stop listening to what your employees are *saying*. Instead of listening to their words, listen to their *feelings*. If you listen to their feelings, you will understand the words and what they mean. This will assist you in becoming a more empathetic listener as well.

Listen to the nonverbal—Yep; listen to what is not being said. This is a hidden secret in understanding intent. We cannot *not* communicate. Our body language conveys a constant story. When body language conflicts with words, it may lead to a different understanding of the message. It is essential to keep eye contact—this not only displays that you're being attentive, but the eyes can't lie. Have you ever faked a smile or displayed a different emotion than you truly felt? I think we've all been in this boat. When someone is speaking to you, watch their eyes—they'll tell you the true story. Other areas to pay attention to include:

1. *The face*—As you watch the face, pay attention to furrowed brows or a jaw that is set. Watch the lips—are they open or pinched closed?

2. *The arms and hands*—Are their arms crossed? This is an indication of defense, nervousness and wanting to protect oneself. Pay attention to the hands; make sure they are not clenched, wringing or fidgety.

3. *The shoulders*—This is another great place to keep your attention. Pay attention to how you keep your shoulders as you process your own emotions. Are they curled, hunched

tense or relaxed? This could be a big indicator of how the person is truly feeling.

The most successful leaders are fluent in understanding nonverbal communication. On a side note, when you are speaking, be aware of your body language as well. Others are paying attention to you.

USE YOUR ABCs

Practice the ABCs—When you're delivering your message, practice the ABCs of good communication: *accuracy, brevity* and *clarity.*

1. *Accuracy*—The message you deliver should always be as accurate as possible. Any time you knowingly give misinformation, you chip away at your leadership integrity. If you ever find out that you gave misinformation, make certain you circle back and correct it. This happens sometimes; fix it by ensuring you give the correct information.

2. *Brevity*—Avoid information overload and deliver your messages as succinctly as possible. That doesn't mean leave out key details; it just means get to the point and give all necessary information to make certain the message can be decoded properly.

3. *Clarity*—To make sure your message is understood, be clear, transparent and free of indistinctness or ambiguity. If time and practicality allow, plan your message beforehand. There is nothing that says all conversations need to be improvised or spur-of-the-moment. Another pearl of wisdom is to watch how others speak and become a student of how they deliver messages.

Open your mind—In a position of leading others, it is imperative that you understand, accept and appreciate everyone as individuals. Leadership means you value the members you've invited to become part of your team. I say this because there are leaders out there who have negative feelings toward their employees stemming from different beliefs, values or understandings. Your workforce does not have to share your personal beliefs, but you have in common the same mission of organizational success. I have coached clients who were biased and had prejudices towards employees. I bring this up under this heading because when you have a preconceived opinion of individuals, it leads you to jump to conclusions, pass judgments and have misunderstandings.

Once you embrace that everyone has their personal beliefs, values and place in the world, it frees the leader to see the value and appreciate the employee. So when you are being spoken to, keep an open mind, listen to the message, engage the communicator and try to learn something you didn't know before they came into your office.

Set the stage—Another thing that is paramount to effective communication is making sure you make yourself available and inviting to members of your team.

When developing into an effective communicator, being someone who can be approached is just as important as understanding any message. You must develop a trust in your workforce that you are a person who wants to hear comments, concerns and ideas—that you are there to help address problems, teach them and help them develop professionally. When someone comes into your office and asks if they can have a minute of your time, that time now belongs to them. Deadlines, projects, e-mails, phone calls, texts—all those distractions need to be eliminated for strong communication to take place. If your office is intimidating, find an alternative place for the conversation to take place. If the conversation takes place in your office, come from behind your desk and sit with the employee—your desk is where you work, not where you lead from.

(I need to give a shout out here: A mentor of mine, Matt Zavadsky of Texas' MedStar Mobile Healthcare, would always do this when anyone went into his office. As his direct report, I would go into his office for support, direction or to share information, and he always came around his desk and sat with me. One time I tried to stop him, saying, "You don't need to come over here." His response was, "Yes, I do," and it is still a very loud answer.)

Take a letter—While speaking and listening skills are vital to your success, a close third is your ability to write letters and e-mails and posts on social media. The world of electronic communication seems rife with poor grammar, misspellings and poor sentence development. Writing skills, if not mastered, can tarnish your leadership ability and damage your reputation. If you have challenges spelling, don't just hit the right word in spell-check. Look at the correct spelling versus your misspelling and learn from your mistake. Spend time with a thesaurus and learn synonyms for words you regularly use. Writing can be a very entertaining process, and I encourage you to start a blog, tell your story, share an anecdote and teach a lesson or skill. Just make certain it's as error-free as possible.

CHAPTER FOUR
Be the Creator of Your Own Opportunity

"If opportunity doesn't knock, build a door."

—Milton Berle

Recently one of my coaching clients made an interesting comment. He is a middle manager in his late 30s, struggling to see the forest for the trees. His comment was based on frustration and started, "They say the U.S. is the land of opportunity. Well, where is my opportunity? Where is my American dream? My ultimate success?"

I have noticed that when people feel frustrated in their life, career or even relationship, the question always seems to come back to "When will I get my break in life?"

There is a quote that says, "Good things come to those who wait," suggesting there are folks just waiting for the opportunities and successes to find them. Nothing could be further from the truth. Maybe some good things come to some of those who wait, but only what is left over from the folks who busted their ass and made things happen and created their own opportunities first.

DEVELOP OPPORTUNITY

In my opinion, waiting for opportunity to come along takes patience and lots of luck, and the reality is that opportunity is slow to come. Instead you should change your thinking and depend solely on yourself as the creator of your own opportunities or successes. This is where you should have a solid vision, goals and plans to create your own success.

SAY YES MORE

The movie *Yes Man* follows the character Carl Allen, played by Jim Carrey. Carl's life is at a standstill, stuck in a rut of the everyday with no real future. After a personal development course that encourages Carl to say yes to every opportunity he encounters, Carl begins to live and experience his life. Saying yes gets him a job promotion, new friends and a new romance. Are you hindering your possible opportunity, your future success by being stagnant in your personal or professional life? Try this experiment for one weekend to start: Say yes to every opportunity that presents itself. Keep yourself out the possibility of becoming the wheelman in a bank robbery. But with that aside, see how being positive to every opportunity changes your weekend. If it makes a difference, try it during the week.

DEVELOP YOUR NETWORK

This is a very important component in developing potential opportunities: The more folks you know and interact with, the greater the likelihood you will begin seeing new experiences. From new experiences comes the potential for developing opportunities. In these days of social media, people are growing their personal and professional networks with thousands of people. One of the challenges, it seems, is that people are losing the ability to meet each other face to face and create their network that way. To counteract this, join groups and become active within your career field. Most fields have professional organizations, periodicals and social media pages. Become active and develop yourself into a subject matter specialist within your realm. Write articles, present at conferences, maybe start your own professional blog to share your experiences with your peers.

ASK MORE QUESTIONS

One of the things I've noticed is that ego plays a big role in business. Ego keeps folks from asking needed questions because they don't want to look like they don't know what they're talking about in front of their peers. If you know everything you need to know about your job or leadership, raise your hand.

There should be no embarrassment in not being familiar with a subject. If this were *The Matrix,* you could just have the program uploaded, and no one would be the wiser. Since that's not possible, your knowledge must derive from experience, mistakes and learning. Asking questions to those in the know is a great way to grow and maybe along the way pick up a mentor.

Asking questions also helps grow your workforce. In place of giving guidance, answers or feedback, ask questions of folks instead. This will help your workforce develop problem-solving and critical-thinking skills. Once you can get your workforce to a place of comfort, they will be more apt to handle situations on their own.

BECOME A RESOURCE

When you take the stance of valuing people, it is normal to extend a hand to help. Let your peers know that if you or your team can be a resource in any way, they should be comfortable asking you. This is a great way to develop opportunities for yourself and your team. As chief of the EMS department for a hospital system in St. Louis, I made it known I could be a resource for anyone who listened. I was asked to be on committees and boards, brainstorm and give my opinions across the 13-hospital system.

Another component is to look out for opportunities for your workforce. I was contacted by a publisher who asked me to write a chapter in a medical reference. With what I had on my plate, I couldn't take this project on in the allotted time frame, so instead I had a member of my leadership team write the needed material. It was one of her goals to be published, and this was an ideal opportunity to accomplish it. As a leader your role is to grow, develop and get your workforce to the next level of their success. Allow them to be resources for organizational opportunities as well.

CONTINUE LEARNING

In his book *The 21 Irrefutable Laws of Leadership,* John Maxwell outlines in the "law of process" that leadership develops daily, not in a day. Modern life has become very "right now"—when we want something, we want it now, and life does all it can to be accommodating as well. We are hungry, there is fast food; we don't even have to leave our cars. Places like Amazon and Wal-Mart are experimenting with two-hour delivery—now I can do my grocery shopping online and have it delivered the same day.

When it comes to your development, leadership knowledge cannot be put into a "right now" format. Growing as a leader cannot be a microwaved process; it takes time to develop, experience and grow your leadership abilities. This is where being a lifelong student comes into play. Try to read something new every day. It could be something about your job, career field or developing your leadership knowledge. What is important is that you choose the topic and spend some time learning. This will help you see available opportunities while increasing your core knowledge.

IS THAT AN OPPORTUNITY?

There are two things to remember here: You can create opportunities, or you can recognize where opportunities exist. What's the best way to put yourself in the best place possible to take advantage of these prospects? It is important to keep in mind the following:

1. The first thing is your mind-set. You learned in Chapter Two that your subconscious mind has a hold on your success. Tell yourself that you want to take advantage of opportunities. Train yourself to be positive, get outside your comfort zone and know that the process of success is found outside everyday habits.

2. Define what you want to achieve. When I talk with clients, I ask what success look like to them, what goals they want to achieve and, most important, what they want their professional legacy to look like at the end of their career. When you understand your goals and desires, it helps outline your blueprint for attaining that success. As opportunities arise that fit into the construction of your blueprint, decisions to pursue those chances become easier to make. Your goal is achieving ultimate success. You are responsible for making that happen.

3. Create a vision of your success or goals. Visualization is a great way to retrain your subconscious mind. As you create a desire for success and that fire to achieve burns and builds, see yourself as if that goal was already achieved. What does that look like for you? How will it help you develop? How does it affect your career? Feel success, enjoy success and allow that visualization to motivate and energize your commitment to achieving your vision. When you follow this exercise, you will see opportunities you've never seen before. Those you encounter will begin to feel your energy and enthusiasm, and that will open doors.

4. Take more risks. I know this is easier said than done. When speaking to audiences I love to ask, "What is the one thing you would do if you knew you would not fail?" I hear some great answers. But it is the fear of failure that keeps people from taking those risks. People stop themselves from taking chances because of the story they tell themselves. Fear is just that: a story you tell yourself. As you believe that story as truth, you cement that mind-set in your subconscious, and it will hinder you for years to come.

5. So, if you knew you would not fail, what would you try? Before you answer, remember that whatever you try in real life, you will make mistakes, have challenges and maybe not succeed. What have you ever mastered when trying it for the first time? Sports? A hobby? Learning something new? In my book *Ultimate Leadership: 10 Rules for Success,* rule No. 7 is "Experience comes from mistakes, and mistakes come from lack of experience." This is a normal process in learning and development. Somewhere in our growth it was decided that mistakes were bad and failure makes us weak. Start to believe the opposite: Mistakes grow your experience, and failures makes you succeed. What is the one thing you would do if you knew you would not fail? Do it and see what happens.

6. Success is contagious. Negative people will suck the life, motivation and desire right out of you. No matter how much you try to keep a positive focus, negative people eventually

wear you down. It is vital for your success to stay positive, motivated and progressing along the path you set for yourself. In surrounding yourself with positive people, you can use them as resource to learn from and brainstorm with. It is no wonder that your environment is crucial to your ability to be happy, focused and successful. Successful people have strong habits and usually make you feel better when you're with them. Attach yourself to like-minded folks and watch your success soar.

7. Use self-reflection to grow. Have you ever spent time wondering why you reacted a certain way? How about reflecting on the progress of a project once it is completed? Self-reflection is an important part of growth and developing the experience needed to continue a path toward success. Put time into your day or week to reflect on how things went, why things happened the way they did and how to change things for the better next time. This will help you gain wisdom, polish experience and grow your foresight and conceptualization in future planning.

You are the creator of your success. No one is going to bring you the success you seek. If you think someone is going to walk into your office and dump an opportunity on your desk or give you ultimate success, you are fooling yourself and wasting time. It is vital to get outside your comfort zone, forge forward and find opportunities that already exist, create your own new opportunities, and keep that momentum always plowing ahead. In closing, George Bernard Shaw has a quote that says, "Life isn't about finding yourself. Life is about creating yourself." Create your life every day.

CHAPTER FIVE
Keep Your Word, Gain Your Trust

"Honor your commitments with integrity."

—Les Brown

One of the most important attributes you need to succeed in life is your word. When you talk, interact and lead people, it's vital they know you say what you mean and, more important, mean what you say. Nothing affects a leader's reputation, trustworthiness and ability to lead more than not being true to their word. In this chapter we outline the importance of developing a solid reputation that will lead you to ultimate success.

CHARACTERISTICS OF A LEADER

Integrity—This is the quality that allows you to be fair and reliable and have a solid moral compass and wholeness of character. The dictionary meaning is *adherence to moral and ethical principles; soundness of moral character; honesty.*

When I was growing up in New York City, my best friend was a cop. He told me of a call he responded to in an apartment complex in the South Bronx. He entered an apartment, and right there in front of him was about $70,000 in cash and narcotics on a table. He arrested a pair of suspects, and while waiting for his partner to show up, one of them told my friend, "Just take all the money and let us go." At the time I was 19 or so and thought, *Man that was a lot of money.* I asked my friend, "What did you do?" Very quickly he responded, "I arrested them and cataloged the narcotics and money."

I looked at him blankly as I processed his response. Then he added, "These folks were breaking the law, and compromising my values and ethics was not worth any amount of money." To me this was an incredible show of integrity. I remember thinking how much I respected my friend for his decision. It gave me comfort that people like him were on the job, keeping us safe.

Trustworthiness—One of the questions I ask when speaking to leaders is this: "How many of you ever had a leader who said they'd get back to you on something but never did?" Usually many hands will go up. Then my follow-up is something like, "How did that make you personally feel?" or "What did you feel about that leader?" This usually opens a great discussion. I allow the group to share their stories, feelings and opinions on the subject.

My next question leads to some somber reflection. "Knowing how your leaders' oversight made you feel," I continue, "how many of you later made a promise to get back to an employee who made a request of you, but then never did?"

As you develop trust in leading your workforce, such an oversight can be very detrimental to your ability to lead. Being trustworthy means developing a reputation of being reliable and following through. Once your words no longer have meaning, your ability to gain followers is lost.

Reputation—What kinds of opinions do people generally hold about you?

In 2010 I became chief of an emergency medical services department. The department once was known as the best in the state, but over the years it had developed a reputation of poor leadership, which led to poor employee engagement and low morale, which eventually led to poor patient care. In my first meeting with the workforce, we discussed a plan to bring the organization back to its days of glory. I remember employees having some reservations, which were outlined to me by several in attendance. My comment to them was clear: "I want you to have reservations. Right now these are just words, and it's up to all of us to work to make it happen." I finished the meeting by saying, "If you follow me, we will become the best EMS agency in the United States." There were some chuckles, sighs and eye-rolling. But over the next couple of years, our leadership team set about making this vision a reality.

Through our personnel's dedication, commitment to excellence and professionalism, this once fractured (I won't say broken) organization was, a few short years later, recognized as the top EMS service in the United States. What do you think would have happened to my reputation if my actions did not support what my bold statement promised?

KEEPING YOUR WORD

In business we are often called upon for information, guidance or to take on a project. We give an assurance, our word, to those who seek from us. When you give your word, it's like writing a verbal check. If that check bounces, trouble always follows. As a leader, those who follow you need to believe in you for vision, strategy and having their best interest in mind. Once you start to default on promises, it begins to chip away at your integrity and reputation.

Your promise leads others to believe you'll deliver what you say. It is that expectation that leads to us forecasting or predicting something will happen. If a group is developing a project for the company and everyone is given a task, others know who's responsible for which deliverables. *We don't have to worry about that report,* they'll think, *because John said he'd do that.* Once that prediction about John fails, though, his coworkers will feel a loss of control. As humans, we always look to gain control. When we feel control is lost, our defense mechanism kicks in and reevaluates whom or what we can trust. To be fair, the opposite is also true: We can also increase our trust as our forecasts are met.

I have known people who make promises very easily, knowing quite well they will never keep them. Let's use this scenario: Someone you like and respect comes to you and asks for assistance. Helping them will take some time. Though your plate is already overflowing, you agree to help, within their allotted timeline.

We often feel an obligation to say yes. The thought *What will they think of me if I say no?* overpowers people. Remember this: You are not saying no to the person, you are saying no to the request. Say, "I would love to help, but I am swamped with several deadlines." Then offer an alternative: "Maybe I can assist in a week or so?"

There are individuals who give their trust effortlessly. These folks can be naïve and are often manipulated and let down. Keep an eye out when this occurs.

There was a client who often talked to me about not being able to help a member on his team. Jeannie was a project manager just out of college, new to the workforce. She was in her mid-20s and looking to make a mark in her first career job. On countless projects, others missed their deadlines, and this caused Jeannie's work to suffer. Instead of holding those who missed their deadlines accountable, she kept believing their excuses ("later today," "tomorrow," etc.). She believed they were busy and would finally come through. They didn't, and eventually Jeannie was coached for missing deadlines and not holding people accountable. She eventually began to have trust issues with her peers, and this caused strain within her circle. Once this occurs, you never look at your peers the same again.

KEEPING PROMISES

Let's look at some tips to assist you in keeping your promises.

1. **Know your capabilities**—At times this may have to come down to making fewer promises. Don't agree so easily or often—the person who always says yes is usually the first person who will get the request. When I worked with an ambulance schedule, it was paramount that ambulances be kept on the street always—it's a 24/7/365 business. When those under my command took off or called in sick, as a young supervisor I would always call the people I knew would fill in on a moment's notice. This of course was good for me; I kept the schedule filled. But it caused challenges with the workforce. The people who were looking for overtime were never called, and those who were being called didn't know how to say no to me and felt I was taking advantage of their off time. What a mess! But it was a valuable lesson for me.

2. **Do it now**—A best practice in over delivering is to complete requests as soon as possible. If you can, make each request the very next task you complete. This practice is good for a couple of reasons: First, it allows you to get back to your associate quickly, and second, it gets that item off your plate—you won't have to worry about it any longer. Now, this task, favor or project still should be completed as professionally and impeccably as possible. I had an employee who always seemed to complete his work with a poor effort, often leaving it inadequate and incomplete. I called him to my office for some coaching and to find out if he was having troubles at work. What I found out was that he didn't know how to say no and instead would complete poor work so he wouldn't be asked any more favors. That's one approach, I guess! You could flip the coin and be known as someone who misses deadlines and breaks their word or someone who does poor work. Either way your reputation is affected.

3. **Are the expectations clear?** —Another challenge is that we don't spend time ensuring we understand what's expected of us. In your head you're concerned about having something else to do and not paying close attention to what's being asked of you. If you give your word to assist someone, take the time to understand what the result is supposed to be. Paraphrase, follow up with an e-mail and do the necessary legwork on the front end to avoid this miscommunication. An ounce of prevention is worth a pound of cure.

4. **Keep the lines of communication open**—When people are relying on you, it's vital you keep them up to date on what's happening. If I was helping an employee with an issue, I'd share what I learned with them at every turn. Letting them know as things happen keeps them in the loop. Otherwise they're wondering, worrying and maybe even losing faith in you. If you're responsible for part of a project, keeping others abreast of your progress lessens the stress on their end. If by some chance you know you're going to miss a deadline, make sure to share that information as soon as you know. One of my biggest pet peeves was when I gave a due date to my

leaders, and when that day arrived they'd tell me they needed more time to complete the request. "When did you know you would miss this deadline?" I would ask. It was always a couple days or longer before. Well, that's when you should have come to me, because on the deadline day I'm expecting your results.

This leads us to the discussion of how best to hold people accountable. Recently I was writing an article on pet peeves in the workplace. Out of more than 100 responses on social media, the No. 1 reader peeve was a lack of accountability in their organization. Second was lack of consistency, which I consider the same.

Holding People Accountable

One characteristic that makes a great leader great is their ability to hold not only their team accountable but also themselves. The art of holding yourself accountable can be overlooked by some leaders. A "do as I say, not as I do" mentality will not keep you in favor with your workforce very long. As a matter of fact, the level of accountability for you and your leadership team should be ratcheted up a couple notches to truly raise the bar.

Let's look at some tips to improve accountability.

1. It goes back to something we discussed a moment ago: Set clear expectations. Most mistakes happen when there's miscommunication, broken communication or even a misunderstanding of expectation. As mentioned above, it's always a best practice to be crystal clear about what you're requesting.

2. Explain why it's important;

3. Outline the request. Based on the employee's experience, you also may have to outline steps or how to complete the task;

4. Ask the employee to paraphrase or share back their understanding of your request.

5. Empower the employee. Now that you've outlined the project or task parameters, make certain they have everything they need to be successful. You may need to delegate your authority, assist with resource-gathering or obtain a special tool for them.

This is a very important step, and not following through could set the employee up for failure.

6. Outline what an excellent outcome looks like. This is something leaders don't do; then when the project is completed, they act surprised with the outcome. Scheduling regular reviews is also important. At time employees are afraid or uncomfortable asking questions or requesting help. This is where regular check-in sessions ensure everything is on track and save lots of wasted time.

7. Ensure there's a clear connection for regular feedback. Maybe this is a task you've given the employee for the first time. This is a great opportunity to help this employee grow. Offer honest and open feedback—it's vital individuals know where they stand in completing their task. Know that first-time mistakes may occur and allow for reflection and teaching to take place.

8. Define the consequences. This is the principal step in holding folks accountable. Now, this does not mean to threaten employees, put fear into them or make them uncomfortable for their positions. But if you're giving them a deadline, outline for them the importance of the deadline—how their failure to meet it will affect the outcome. It's acceptable to say something like, "I am trusting you that this will be completed on time." To really drive the point home, "Failure to complete this task on time may result in me asking someone else next time." Remember, our role as leaders is to get the very best out of our workforce. You need to teach, motivate and inspire them every step of the way.

DEVELOPING YOUR REPUTATION

Your word as a leader must be the one constant that can never fluctuate. It is keeping your pledge—acting in support of your words—that shapes what others will say about you. This is the foundation of developing an unquestionable reputation. Here are some tips to consider when advancing your reputation:

1. **It's all about what you say**—Your role as a leader is to get the best out of the folks you're charged to lead. It sounds like a simple task, but sometimes leaders get caught up with other responsibilities, and even the easiest of requests can go overlooked. Your workforce, peers, customers and clients must know you will meet their deadlines and deliver what you said you would. Your goal should be to become this person.

2. **Become a resource to others**—One of the responsibilities of leadership is to help others reach their goals, guide them to the next level and be the source of making things happen. How many times have you needed help, been stuck on a project or not known where to go next? This is where your assistance to others truly makes the difference. Being known as the go-to person will allow you to become an invaluable source in making others successful.

3. **Help others look good**—Today it seems many people try to get ahead by making others look bad. Maybe they're after your position; they may bad-mouth you to the workforce or maybe even your boss. This practice has no place in the business world and carries very challenging consequences. Instead of stabbing backs, make it your practice to make everyone look the best they can. It should be your plan to think every day about how you can add value, share responsibility or just make others feel important. Make the effort to put others in the spotlight, make key introductions and share the knowledge that will grow their experiences.

4. **Under promise and over deliver**—The key to success not only for a leader but in business is to get people to know, like and trust you. One of the ways to do this is to under promise and over deliver. If you say you'll get back to someone in a day, make it hours. Send handwritten thank-you notes and make small gestures to individuals who go above and beyond what's expected. This will strengthen your value to others and lend great momentum to building your reputation.

5. **Be consistent**—It's all about consistency. One of the things I hear most when consulting with organizations is personnel

talking about favoritism, not being treated fairly or even that the leadership just doesn't like them. This is a result of inconsistency and sometimes even preconceived judgment toward individuals. It is vital to developing your reputation that people will know exactly how decisions will be made and carried out, and that they always be the same. It is easy to change a decision for employees we're fond of, but the employee you're accommodating will question your motives, as will other employees who will also eventually question your loyalty to them. When facing a situation you've faced before, you should make the same decision. If a decision is being made for the first time, sit with your leadership team and seek input on how to handle the situation. Do this with an understanding that this is how you'll respond to the same situation in the future.

6. **But be flexible**—With that said, sometimes you may need to change how you handle a situation. If this occurs, it is vital you share with your workforce why this decision is being changed. Maybe it's something as easy as "We had this situation arise in the past, and this was our response. We now have some additional information that will cause us to change our practice in the future." Then outline the new process, decision or action so there is no misunderstanding as to why things are different going forward.

7. **Be engaging**—There are many people out there who just can't stand their boss. To be honest I've been in this position myself, and I'm sure there have been folks in my career who didn't like my decisions. This happens, but for the most part employees want to work for someone they respect—someone whom they know cares about them and has their best interests in mind. Make it a practice to enjoy conversation, be approachable and likable, and make time to hear concerns, comments and suggestions. If you expect to have an engaged workforce, it should be your mission to engage with them as well.

8. **Be a teacher**—Learning should be a never-ending practice for the successful professional. It is vital that you keep up on your industry, focus on upcoming changes and share

them with your workforce. Over my 30 years, the healthcare environment seemed it was a never-ending quagmire of change. Being able to stay up on what was happening in my field, share new directions, teach new skills and mentor folks helped me equip my workforce to deliver the highest quality of patient care possible. Develop an organizational culture that believes in learning, and you as the leader become their teacher. One good practice is to become a thought leader in your field. Being an expert makes teaching easier. Make the effort to write articles, develop a blog and develop presentations to deliver at conferences.

9. **Ask for feedback**—The people doing the work want to be part of the vision and organizational success. Being stuck in their work space and just told to do the work is not their idea of being on a winning team. There are people who have ideas, suggestions and experiences they'd like to share. Create brainstorming sessions, ask their opinions and allow them to help you solve problems. You'll be surprised at the conversations and suggestions that result. Another component is asking them about you as a leader. A practice I had when a member of the workforce came to my office was to ask them one of four questions:

   1. *What suggestions do you have for me to be a better leader to you?* Just because you're leading folks doesn't mean it's working for them, allow them to guide you in a style that does.

   2. *If you were in charge, what's the one thing you would change and why?* This will help you take the pulse of your workforce. If you hear about a problem or area of concern, do your homework, determine a root cause and address it as necessary.

   3. *What can I do for you today?* When individuals seek your counsel, depending on their personalities, it may be difficult for them to share their concerns, comments or suggestions. This question opens the door and conveys that you're prepared to do something for them.

4. *Where are you in reaching your goals?* It's a leader's responsibility to make certain the workforce is growing. Goal-setting is a big part of that growth. If you can assist in any way—be a resource, make an introduction or knock down a barrier for them—do it. This will solidify that your charge is to help them develop into the best professional possible.

REPAIRING YOUR REPUTATION

A reputation takes a long time to develop and a short time to destroy. Destruction can happen by misunderstanding, making the wrong choices or trying to cut corners. In my career I made decisions that cost me respect and even tarnished my reputation.

One day when I was feeling the frustration of my responsibilities, an employee made a boneheaded mistake. I allowed my emotions to dictate my response and yelled at that employee in front of other employees. It was an ultimate embarrassment for me, and my leadership integrity and reputation took a horrible beating. This error in judgment caused me challenges for about five years. I can share that my onetime standing never quite bounced all the way back.

There are times when these things will pop up, and you may need to consider some damage control and reconstruct your leadership reputation.

Admit your mistake—This is the first thing, even before the words "I'm sorry" surface. Standing in front of your workforce, admitting your mistake, explaining how it occurred, saying it will never happen again, then delivering a heartfelt apology can begin the healing process. Remember, just because you took these steps doesn't mean everything will be OK thereafter. You must once again begin the climb back into your workers' good graces and being someone who can be trusted and followed.

Humility is a must—You may have had a great reputation, maybe larger than life. When it comes to reconstructing your reputation, it is paramount you be humble and show your true feelings. We all make mistakes, and you are no different. You are falling on your sword, and it hurts; show them how you truly feel.

Always stay positive—This can be a frustrating time, and becoming discouraged can happen easily. Once you begin the rehabilitation of your reputation, it takes a marathon of time to repair it. Keep your head up and allow a positive behavior to become contagious. Continue with positive communication as well. You may not feel like engaging in meetings or brainstorming sessions. Keep your focus, remember who you are and contribute as before. As you go through this process, you may have the tendency to beat yourself up because of the situation you're in. Once you begin to rectify it, move forward, stay focused and forge back toward the good graces of your peers.

CHAPTER SIX
Experience Your Failures

"Your attitude toward failure determines your altitude after failure."

—John C. Maxwell

As a young boy in New York City, I accidently used the *F* word. My Italian mother heard me and came running, screaming at me at the top of her lungs. "I cannot believe what I just heard!" she yelled. "Where did you learn such a horrible word?! You are so much better than that! In this family no one will ever use that word!"

I wanted to crawl under a rock to escape the horrible embarrassment.

Now pointing her finger at me, my mother said, "*Failure* is the worst *F* word ever used to describe us or our lack of accomplishments. If you say it, and truly believe you're a failure, that's what you will become."

She concluded by saying, "Failure is never an option." Then she kissed me and slapped the back of my head. At this early age I'd just experienced some tough love. I may have gotten off easier if I was caught using the bad four-letter *F* word instead.

Though we will be discussing failures and mistakes, I wanted to spend some time discussing fear. The mentality we have about failure and mistakes is backward. When we were children, getting that tough love when mistakes were made was burned into our subconscious with a hot iron. Unfortunately this scar can cause folks to believe that making mistakes has no place in our growth and development. The intended lesson backfires, and recipients develop two results they often continue to carry: a fear of failure and a fear of disapproval

FEAR DEFINED

When I talk to people as part of my coaching duties, I always get around to asking their definition of fear. Most of the time there is no clear-cut definition. For our discussion we will define fear as *an objectionable feeling of trepidation or concern when you perceive something alarming, hazardous or destructive may arise.*

Fear of failure is the biggest hindrance to achievement and eventual success. Due to this fear of failure, individuals make excuses and refuse to leave the safety of their comfort zone. To keep you safe, your subconscious can create debilitating self-talk worthy of an Academy Award. When you consider stepping outside to try something new, it slaps you right back to reality with a story of fear and failure.

The key word in that last sentence is *story*. Think about it: Fear is just a story you tell yourself. When you tell yourself this story, it creates the feeling of fear. Now what you're fearing is less failure itself than just the uncomfortable feeling fear brings.

The fear story places you in what I like to call the *box of fear*. This is your own little mental prison. When the feeling of fear strikes, you feel alone, confined, scared and not sure what to do next. It's almost like your own little solitary confinement. Usually you enter the "box" when something triggers your fear. This trigger can be real or something perceived. From there the trigger stimulates a response. This response can be physical, mental or both. This can make people susceptible to anxiety attacks. After the negative feelings, you begin to exhibit behaviors that ultimately sabotage your intentions.

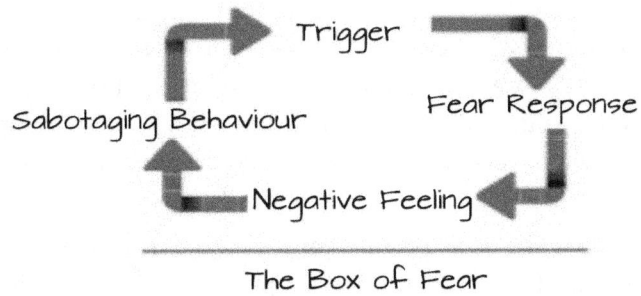

The Box of Fear

THE PURPOSE OF FEAR

Fear does have a purpose; it's what keeps us safe. Consider fear as the fuse to our parasympathetic nervous system, which produces our fight-or-flight response. It tells us to either put our hands up or set a record for the 100-yard dash. It prompts our body to an appropriate state of readiness.

When a perceived threat is just imagination, your mind cannot differentiate if it's a real threat or creation. It just knows there's a threat, and your parasympathetic nervous system takes over to protect you. This is an important factor in how your story or perceived threat affects you physically. Back in Chapter Two we discussed how your subconscious mind couldn't evaluate, reject or disregard an idea; it only accepts what you're telling it to be true. So with whatever truth you believe, your subconscious mind begins developing a plan to eliminate the threat.

What is unfortunate here is that unlike an actual threat, which may resolve itself in time, this mental threat is a constant and produces scary thoughts forever. Remember, if you determine a threat is real, you'll stay focused on that threat constantly for your own self-preservation. If you keep thinking about this fear, it keeps you in that box. It triggers and enables negative feelings and causes you to sabotage your success. It's a cycle that won't end until you determine it's time.

TAKING CONTROL OF YOUR FEAR

Now that we know that, how can you take control of your fear? It's a good thing you're still interested, because this is where we head next.

I have a friend who gets very uncomfortable with the thought of riding roller coasters. She has three daughters who are daredevils and never want to get off these thrill rides. They visit theme parks as a family, and whenever their trips are planned, the daughters require that my friend must ride at least one big roller coaster.

Naturally the thought of this causes trepidation every time the subject comes up. It's easy to say, "Well, just don't think about it." But trying not to think about the fear of riding the roller coaster doesn't work. You tell yourself not to think about what you're thinking about, and boom, you enter the box of fear.

In its place you must be able to break the cycle of fear, and that only occurs by taking control and escaping your mental prison. It's not about fear, anxiety or even what you think may happen. What you can control is the thoughts you have about your potential fear.

It's not like someone is standing there with a gun asking for your money. (In that situation I'd hand over my wallet as two drops of pee came out!) That's scary, but remember, this is a story you're telling yourself. This is your imagination causing your subconscious mind to react.

FACING YOUR FEARS

So if we head back to riding the roller coaster, what's the fear here? Is it falling out? The speed? Twists? Turns? Going upside down? It could be any one of those things. It could also be the feeling of not being in control, being at the mercy of the person operating the ride. This fear is based on an uncertainty; you just don't know the outcome. The secret here is to believe in yourself. You must cultivate this belief and trust yourself to handle whatever situation arises.

I know that's easier said than done, but when you replace those negative thoughts with positive ones, you'll notice you're doing more things you imagined. You may have to start small: List the things you fear and determine a way to ease into facing them. It's OK to feel the fear; in my book *Ultimate Leadership: 10 Rules for Success*, when discussing fear, I used an analogy: You feel hot, you feel cold, you feel hungry, and when you have those feelings, you take positive steps to address them. When you feel afraid, it's the same story: Make the decisions necessary to produce the needed outcome.

Just one more thought before we move on to addressing mistakes and failures: With any fear—say, riding roller coasters—comes reflection that leads to self-criticism. There is a ton of research out there that finds self-criticism eventually leads to depression. The more you criticize, the more depressed you can become. It is vital for your mental health to stay positive, surround yourself with supportive people and find the needed strength to conquer your fearful thoughts.

As a P.S. to this section, my friend went on holiday to Universal Studios and rode one roller coaster four times. So there is hope!

MISTAKES AT WORK

Fear of failure is the usual catalyst for folks not stepping outside their comfort zones. Not wanting to make mistakes keeps them inside their cocoon of safety. Beyond that cocoon are people scarfing up opportunities and promotions.

Name one thing you were 100% successful with the first time you tried. Any time we step out to try something new, there's always a learning curve—something we overlook, something we didn't know. And sometimes the mistakes we make teach us what not to do next time.

Growing up in New York City was always educational in some form or fashion. I remember one of the older boys telling me to be a member of their club, I had to put my tongue on the spark plug of his minibike. I did, but not only was I not allowed in the club, I never put my tongue on the spark plug of a minibike again.

In my Air Force days, there was always some hazing with the younger guys. This led to my introduction to the dreaded snipe hunt. A snipe was a fictitious bird that could only be caught at night. See, a snipe hunt takes three guys: Two guys chase the snipe toward the third guy, who's holding the bag and repeating as loudly as possible, "Snipe! Snipe! Snipe!" Well, come to find out (but only after a good hour of losing my voice) there is no such thing as a snipe. Mistake—never go on a snipe hunt again. At least not as the bagman.

More to our topic, when I began my own business, it was vital to learn all the ins and outs of running one successfully. When you work for yourself, there's lots to learn and master. This was a big curve, and tons of mistakes were made.

Learning the science of social marketing, for instance, included several figurative kicks to the groin until I learned the errors of my ways. Every time I thought I'd developed a great ad, I forgot this or didn't do that. It honestly took six times or more to give me my education. During this time I remember having some negative thoughts about my abilities, but recalling that this was my first adventure in learning this new task grounded me.

The lesson here on all accounts is that there is no success without failure. One of my favorite quotes comes from Michael Jordan, who said, "I've missed more than 9,000 shots in my career. I've lost almost 300 games. Twenty-six times I've been trusted to take the game-winning shot and missed. I've failed over and over and over again in my life. And that is why I succeed."

There are countless stories from history, business, sports and every aspect of life of failure leading toward success. A good one involves a comedian—he wanted to be as big as they came. He developed a set of jokes and received his first opportunity to wow an audience. His big chance came—he was introduced, walked out on stage, looked at the audience and...froze. He was eventually booed and jeered off stage. This would have devastated most people, but the next evening he came right back and completed his set to laughter and applause. From there he had a great career and eventually developed a show you may have heard of: *Seinfeld*.

Then there was the young man who in his early years was told by his teachers he was "too stupid to learn anything." When he eventually went to work, he was fired from his first two jobs for not being productive enough. Even after he found his calling, he made hundreds of mistakes before finding the right combination that led to the development of...the light bulb. Of course we are talking about Thomas Edison.

Are you worried about leaving your comfort zone? How do you know you're not like the folks above—destined for greatness, something historical, developing something we could all benefit from? That may seem far-fetched, but do you *know* you're not destined to be placed right in the middle of history?

In my career I was trained as a paramedic. It was my duty to be the best part of someone's worst day. As my career progressed I attained the rank of chief and led my own department. One mundane summer day, as I was going about my daily duties, I found myself right in the middle of an international spotlight focused on Ferguson, Mo. Certainly this was not an event that was expected, and along the way my department (and all of us) experienced mistakes, failures and lessons learned en route to overall success. But the point I want to make here is this: You never know how your contribution will make the difference to yourself, your organization, mankind or history.

MAKING MISTAKES, HAVING FAILURES

Say it with me: It takes failure after failure to produce success. This should be your mantra moving forward. What's the one thing you'd do if you knew you wouldn't fail? Take a moment, think about it. Maybe it's a new hobby, learning a new software program or changing your career path. What is your one thing? Write it below.

_____

_____

_____

_____

_____

_____

Now spend a moment thinking about what this achievement would mean to you. What if you knew you may fail at it one time— would you still do it? Maybe, just maybe, you'll fail at it two or three times, but along the way you'll eventually become the best you can be. Would you still do it?

Let's look at some steps to dealing with mistakes:

1. **It's not the end of the world**—Mistakes are a normal part of life, growth, development and education. Mistakes come from lack of experience; experience comes from mistakes.

When you make a mistake, you may want to hide in a corner and wallow in self-pity. Well, if that's how you want to address it initially, give yourself some time to feel bad, then move on. Once you move on, don't wear that mistake or failure as a badge of honor. You are a professional, not a historian.

2. **Stay positive**—When mistakes happen, spend some time reflecting on what went wrong, how you can make it better and what it taught you. On another note, once you get the lesson, share it with people on your team. Let everyone benefit from the experience.

3. **Try just one more time**—You want to guarantee your success? Try just one more time. The word is *persistence*—keep forging forward, try it differently, learn from mistakes. Don't give up on that something you want to achieve.

4. **Your mistakes do not make you a failure**—Making mistakes doesn't mean you're a failure. Mistakes do not define you and are not the foundation of who you are. Such is life, and in all my years I still have not found the instruction manual for living it. Until that manual is excavated from a tomb in some desert, we just should keep plowing along. Mistakes will happen, and that's OK.

5. **Apologize as necessary**—Sometimes there may be the need to say you're sorry. This is just the way of life: We do things with the best of intentions, and sometimes we screw the pooch. If you know you'll be making mistakes, be ready to admit when you do. Be honest, take responsibility and let the chips fall where they may. Another note here: Never, ever blame someone else for your mistake. If it belongs to you, own it; and second, always take the blame for mistakes your team makes.

This is the essence of life: We wake up, go to work, live life, make mistakes. It's a normal part of existence. So back away from the thought and fear that mistakes and failures are the boogeyman. Know that the greatest people in history—your parents, mentors, brothers, sisters, peers and the rest of society—have all made mistakes and learned from their failures.

CHAPTER SEVEN
Leaders Make Mistakes Too

"Failure is simply the opportunity to begin again, this time more intelligently."

—Henry Ford

One of my favorite topics to speak on is the 10 most common leadership mistakes. Yes, it's true: Leaders make mistakes too. These mistakes will hinder, challenge and incapacitate your success. Mistakes will come; if you learn from them, you will remember them, avoid repeating them and develop into a better leader because of them.

10. NOT DELEGATING AUTHORITY

This mistake stems from not separating the worker and leader mentalities. As a worker who does an amazing job, you decide to throw your hat in the ring for an open supervisor position. Through the luck of the Irish, you are chosen for this position. Now comes the task of learning the skill set needed to be a great leader. Unfortunately, without the proper training and leadership development, the only skill set you possess is that of a worker. As you go through your new leadership responsibilities, you are still in a worker's mind-set. The feeling that you still must do all the work is fresh in your mind. This derails your ability to effectively lead your workforce.

DELEGATION OF AUTHORITY DEFINED

Delegation of authority extends your authority and empowerment to members of your team. By giving them your authority, you are trusting others to assist you with some of your responsibilities to achieve maximum program results.

When using your power of delegation, you should be aware of the components of delegating. These include authority, responsibility and accountability.

Authority—Authority is the influence needed to use resources proficiently to achieve organizational objectives. When using your authority, it is vital that boundaries are well defined and not crossed. Abusing your authority is a surefire way to lose followers and damage your leadership credibility. Authority cascades from top to bottom positions and is essential to organizational success. When sharing your authority, you must ensure you use equal amounts of responsibility as well.

Responsibility—When you share your authority, the person with the highest authority is still holds ultimate responsibility. If you decide to include a member of your workforce in a project assigned to you and that team member drops the ball, you should not throw that employee under the bus. The ultimate responsibility is yours. One mistake leaders make is to share responsibility but not authority. If you decide to give me some project responsibility but not allow me to have any influence, my ability to be successful is hampered. Responsibility and authority go hand in hand.

Accountability—Recently I conducted a poll where I asked 800 participants their biggest pet peeve at work. The No. 1 answer was the lack of accountability within their organizations. That is more of a systemic organizational problem. For the purposes of delegating authority, you have shared your authority and given responsibilities; now you must develop and hold individuals accountable. Accountability grows from seeds of responsibility—it means you're answerable for the outcome and final results. When it comes to organizational success, accountability cannot be avoided.

The secret recipe for delegating authority is to share tasks and duties, assign your authority with a sprinkle of empowerment, and mix in accountability for assigned responsibilities.

A Vital Skill

Is delegation of authority important to your success as a leader? The short and long of it is yes. At times your roles and responsibilities will reach your capacity and overflow your plate. This is where you need a systematic approach for sharing duties. Sharing my authority with my personnel gives me the opportunity to multiply myself while growing my workforce.

As a leader, sharing work responsibilities decreases your workload and allows you to focus on other areas. This allows you to bring effectiveness, address problems and critical issues, and focus your efforts on developing your workforce.

How to Delegate Authority

The first step in delegating authority lies in planning. This step is often overlooked and a cause of failure. As you foster the plan to delegate a task, determine who might receive this opportunity. Examine their skill set and determine what tools they will need to be successful. Are they seasoned employees, or is this a new task for them? Outline the goals of the task and how outcomes will be measured.

This should be your opportunity to develop a blueprint for success. For the sake of time, leaders often just throw a project or task at an employee and go along their merry way. But remember, as you delegate this task, you are ultimately responsible for its outcome. Developing a plan for success not only sets the employee up for success but you as well.

Once your blueprint is complete, spend an abundant amount of time sharing the plan. This step will lay the perfect foundation for success. Allow for discussion, questions and training if needed. During this period it is vital to confirm your commitment to the outcomes expected and outline timelines and deadlines.

An additional thing to be conscious about is micromanaging during this process. Nothing will turn an employee off more than standing over them and breathing down their neck. Once you determine this task belongs to someone, allow them the autonomy to see it through. You've already set up a blueprint for success; now set up regular check-in sessions. These could be formal meetings, pop-in checks, whatever works for the situation.

TOP DELEGATION FAILURES

If delegation is such an important factor to organizational success, why is it one of the top 10 most common leadership mistakes? Great question! Let's examine that very thing.

Loss of control—Sometimes ego plays a big role in how leaders act in the workplace (later in this chapter we'll examine this a bit more). Other times there's just a feeling that your way is the best way to get things done. Early in my career I had the opportunity to be a field training officer. It was my responsibility to familiarize, train and acclimate new paramedics entering our organization. As a paramedic intent on delivering the highest quality of patient care possible, my routines were set, and of course in my mind they were best practices. The challenge came when other paramedics had their routines: I often scorned them and tried to get them to do it my way. I wanted to control my truck and how the patients received care. Fortunately it was not long until I recognized my error. A bit of ego and lots of wanting to be in control did not allow me to delegate as appropriately as I should have. A basic factor in leadership is learning to give up control—if you can't do it, you're not a leader.

Getting recognition—Everyone loves a good pat on the back and to be recognized for doing a job well. Leaders must begin to delegate tasks they once were praised for completing themselves. Let's blow the lid off this fallacy right now: Say you were great at getting a report out a week before it was due every month. In the monthly meeting you were recognized by the boss in front of your peers. Now, as you take on more responsibilities in a leadership role, you need to pass the preparation of that report off to another member of your team. Now they'll be getting the praise for getting it done a week before it's due. But remember, you are their leader, and you are ensuring and creating the circumstances under which this report is being completed. True, your teammate is getting the credit you once received, but you allowed that to happen for them. Have you ever been told, when someone was impressed with your work, "I wish I had more of you!"? Well, you're creating more of you, and that's even more important than completing the report a week early.

"But I enjoy that!"—There are always areas of responsibility you like to complete personally. You relish tackling a task and have high expectations for its completion. But now you have new responsibilities and need to hand that task off. Just like above, you wanted to be a leader, and that brings you different tasks to learn to love. As you delegate the task you once loved, share the whys and how's and help grow the next generation.

"I'm the best!"—Another big failure is thinking no one can do it better than you. How did you get great at doing that thing? Were you great at it from the very beginning, or was it over time that you honed your skills? Just because someone is new, does it differently or doesn't follow your practice doesn't mean they're wrong. They're just different, and if the results are the same, does it matter? (With this said, there are some tasks that need to be done in certain ways to meet appropriate practice and compliance.)

"They won't need me!"— "If I give up this task, then why do they need me any longer?" This was a question one of my coaching clients asked me a couple months back. Jack was in his late 20s and had just been promoted to a front-line supervisor position. There were tasks Jack needed to complete that he just could not get done. As he delegated those tasks, he became fearful it would be perceived he wasn't doing his job and the organization wouldn't need him any longer. As we worked together it was vital for Jack to realize that as you delegate to others and they complete work at a high level, more things are getting completed, and this will lead to recognition. Another factor is that you are teaching other members of your team how to complete tasks different from their regular duties. This is a win-win for everyone.

Trust—Lacking confidence in your team is truly a big problem, but the problem is yours. You must find ways to develop that trust, teach new skills, coach and learn to become comfortable with trusting folks. Your success as a leader depends on being able to delegate to them. Delegate tasks to the right people and allow them to wow you with their results. Sometimes those results will be subpar, and this is where your ability to teach, coach and grow that team member comes in handy.

9. Not Setting Goals with Employees

Our ultimate responsibility as leaders is to get the very best out of our workforces. From the beginning we set up hiring processes, interviews and personality testing. Hiring managers sit across from potential employees and try to select the right fit for the position. Once you choose the best candidate to fill your opening, does your responsibility stop there? No, new employees come to us with specific experiences and skill sets. It is the responsibility of the leader to polish each skill set, teach new skills and grow more experience.

Keep in mind that you're inviting employees into your organization to help you and your organization become successful. If you don't set goals with members of your team, they do not grow; they'll become stagnant and eventually look for other positions. Now we're back to the hiring process again. People do not quit organizations; people quit their leaders. It is vital that you continue to teach, polish, challenge and grow your workforce. Getting the best out of them means you must add value to them and help them reach the next level in their professional skill set. Therefore, setting goals with employees is a fundamental obligation to the success of the employee, you as the leader and ultimately the organization.

Setting Goals

Setting goals with your workforce allows you to accompany each teammate on their professional development journey. When you give that employee hope and ideas for a better future, this not only helps them but eventually the clients and customers they serve.

Make time to visit and chat with your workforce to determine what goals mean the most to them. Sometimes these may be mutual goals; other times they may be the employee's goal. Regardless, make the time regularly to help your personnel set, evaluate and reach professional goals. As employees journey toward their goals, they become stronger and better at what they're doing.

Is the Concept SMART?

As we begin to discuss the concept of SMART goals, I'd like to take some time to talk about the foundation of the idea. When we think about modern organizational management, one of the world's most persuasive leaders was Dr. Peter Drucker. Drucker's work revolutionized corporate management in the 1950s.

In his 1954 book *The Practice of Management,* Drucker introduced the world to the concept of "management by objectives" (MBO). This groundbreaking work transformed leadership and management into a specialty that is still taught in business schools and practiced in organizations every day.

The philosophy behind MBO deals with the interaction between the manager and his team. They work jointly to advance the organization through pursuit of agreed-upon objectives. Drucker's concepts outlined how various organizational hierarchies need to be integrated, the importance of commitment, responsibility and maturity, and the need for common challenge. These factors help the workforce understand what's expected of them to reach organizational success. Extending the concept allows individuals to set their own goals.

A best practice for any organization is strategic planning. Once you've set a plan, you must develop goals to make the plan come to life. It is vital that every level of management identifies goals and how they fit into the big picture.

Remember that the link between setting an organization's direction and reaching its goals deals with the performance of the workforce. It is here the concept of SMART goals arises.

SMART is an acronym that reminds you of the areas to address in goal development:

SMART for Goal Setting

S - Specific

M - Measurable

A - Attainable

R - Realistic

T - Time

1. **Specific**—Many times organizations don't focus on specific areas for goal completion. When developing goals be specific about the result you wish to attain. Instead of creating a goal to "increase employee engagement," the goal should be to be to "increase employee engagement by 10%." Another element of this is to determine all the specifics involved in making the goal a reality. Outline why the goal is important, who will be involved in accomplishing it, what resources will be needed and who has overall responsibility.

2. **Measurable**—Once a goal is specified, focus on if it's measurable. This will allow you to gauge progress and keep the team focused. Tracking progress allows those doing the work to see how they're impacting success, which keeps motivation high. Another component of measurability is knowing where you're starting from and what an acceptable cap is. In the emergency medical services field, it was crucial that ambulances arrived on scene for life-threatening calls in less than nine minutes 90% of the time (a common industry benchmark). Setting measurable goals gave us a foundation for achieving measurable results. If we fell short, we knew exactly what was expected and made changes to better achieve it. When focusing on this element, ask the questions "how much?" and "how many?"—this will give you a sense of what constitutes reaching the goal.

3. **Attainable**—This is a very important element: Any goal you outline to reach needs to be attainable. Make no mistake, it should stretch your abilities, but ultimately it should be achievable. Setting unattainable goals will demotivate the folks trying to attain them. When developing this element consider why you're in your current position. Using the ambulance example above, if your response times average 10 minutes or compliance rate is 80%, investigate why.

4. **Realistic**— *Realistic* and *attainable* go hand in hand. Ask why this goal matters, how it fits into the vision and plan. Realistic goals drive motivation. Always ask if a goal is meaningful

and if it will be counterproductive to other departmental or organizational goals.

5. **Time**—A goal is a dream with a deadline. It is paramount that you put a time limit on achieving your outcome. As a good rule of thumb, have goals that are quarterly, semiannual and annual. Any time frame works; just ensure you set one. It's also a best practice to periodically share where you are in achieving goals. If you're looking to increase sales by 20% in six months, share monthly milestones with the workforce. People should never be wondering where they stand. Know when things need to be completed and schedule regular check-ins to make certain you're on target.

It makes no difference if you're setting departmental, organizational or personal goals, the SMART method allows you to be successful in the end.

8. Not Treating Employees Fairly

The secret to building trust with employees is being consistent and treating everyone fairly. What you do for one is what the others should expect as well. Failure to do so shows favoritism and is a surefire way to build dissent. Treating employees fairly and without bias will allow you to build relationships, connections and respect with your workforce. Developing a culture of trust and respect reflects directly on employee engagement, satisfaction and retention.

There's a difference between treating employees fairly and treating employees equally. One mistake I made in my career related to treating all employees equally. Our organization was giving modest raises averaging 1.5% per worker, but department managers could divvy out their pool of money as they saw appropriate within their department. If I'd wanted to, I could have given my high performers 2.5%, the middle performers 1.5% and the low performers 0.5%—it would have worked out the same. But my approach was to give all employees 1.5% increases. This was such a small amount, I didn't think it would matter. Well, the next year we were scheduled once again to receive 1.5% raises. I prepared to take the same approach until some of the high performers questioned it. With this structure, they asked, where was the incentive to stay a high performer? Lesson learned—I changed the structure to award a bit more to those who were highly engaged and performed to a higher standard.

7. Not Continuing to Learn

What got you through the door may not keep you in the room. As individuals seek promotion, they invest preparation, hard work and focus. During this time they do everything possible to get an upper hand on getting that promotion. Once that promotion is attained, though, the learning often slows or stops. One of the biggest challenges leaders face is not taking the time necessary to continue their professional growth. Just because you're in a leadership position doesn't mean you're free and clear of the learning environment. In fact, it doubles the amount of continuing education and professional development you should be putting in.

Living in St. Louis, I've become a rabid fan of the St. Louis Blues pro hockey team. Ken Hitchcock, their coach from 2011–2017, was someone I watched, supported and admired. In 2016 Ken said 2017 would be his last year coaching the Blues. This disappointed the team's fans; the team had done well under his leadership, drawing closer each year to a championship. But Hitchcock's reason made perfect sense. He said in his press conference, "To stay a competitive coach, I need to take classes in the off-season." He felt these classes helped maintain his competitive edge, and if he couldn't complete them, he wouldn't be able to give his job the best he had.

Learn How?

Become a student of your career field. Read journals, research and any other data that will help you forecast and conceptualize the future of your field. From there write articles. Find out what you need to do to get published in those journals. As you prepare to write, you will need to research, maybe interview, and gather information that will help you to deliver the best article possible.

Draw from others' best practices. Belonging to professional groups and having a peer network can help you learn how others handle problems in their organizations. This peer network should consist of individuals both inside and outside your field. This group of professionals can act as your sounding board and give guidance as needed. Along those lines, make efforts to find a mentor. Mentors are a wealth of information, experience and expertise. Allow their years of experience to help you learn and grow to the next level.

Prepare to make mistakes and learn from them. I can't even estimate how many boneheaded mistakes I've made in my career. Some have been very costly to my reputation and effectiveness as a leader. But those errors and failures taught me lessons on my way to becoming a better leader.

There is another resource to consider learning from, and that is your workforce. You have a surplus of expertise, knowledge and skill working on your teams. Ask them for their opinions on how to do the best job possible.

Your leadership development is not a sprint; it's a marathon, and you're always on mile 10. Stay focused on the horizon and oriented to growth.

6. NOT GETTING TO KNOW YOUR EMPLOYEES

The way organizations go about dealing with employees is based on tradition and old thinking. Your workforce is on the front lines of bringing ultimate success to your organization. When I visit with organizations having employee satisfaction and engagement challenges, the catalysts usually involve poor leadership, poor communication and disregard, really, for the workforce as a resource.

Remember that you invited these individuals into your organization to help you be successful. It is vital to leadership and organizational success to do everything you can to help them grow, guide them and help them develop into the best professionals they can become.

Take the time to develop professional relationships with your team. One question I like to ask in my speaking engagements is, "How many of your employees have families?" Several hands go up. Then the next question drops them quickly: "What are their names?"

Your workforce chose to work with you to help support their families and way of life. They chose your company to interview, and you chose them because you thought they'd be the best fit. But what motivates your employees? What inspires them? What are their goals? What do they want out of their careers?

These are all things a great leader needs to know. There is an adage that is true: Employees do not quit organizations, they quit other people. If leaders want to develop an employee-retention program that works, here is the recipe: Get to know your employees, listen to them, appreciate them, add value to them every day, help them reach their goals and respect their work-life balance.

When you get to know your employees and what fuels their fire, it helps you as a leader to get the very best out of them. In turn those employees are motivated to develop into the best professionals they can become. No one wants to work where they feel restricted; individuals want to be creative, feel safe and know their efforts are appreciated.

Within organizations there is a lot of time spent communicating expectations to the workforce. How much time does your organization spend analyzing what the workforce expects from their leaders? Here are a few things to consider.

1. Individuals enjoy and thirst for recognition. It is imperative that as the leader you find ways to acknowledge hard work and achievements. Give deserved credit, celebrate milestones, make them feel important to the company. Get into the habit of sending handwritten thank-you notes. Remember, some individuals like to receive praise in a group, others are more private. Give positive feedback where they are most comfortable. How will you know that? By getting to know your employees.

2. Treat them with respect and be polite. How did you wish to be treated when you were a worker? One question I like to ask when conducting leadership training is, "Would you work for you?" This is the golden rule: Treat people as you wish to be treated. People who are treated with respect are more likely to share ideas, be creative and push themselves to work hard. This will increase your credibility and reputation as a solid leader.

3. They want to follow someone who models the way. You are their role model and possibly mentor. It is crucial for success that you live to the standards of professionalism, behavior and dedication you expect from them. The "do as I say, not as I do" mentality does not work, but "what you permit, you promote" is true.

4. The expect transparency from their leaders and organizations. This is their organization too, and it's a good practice to share, as possible, what's going on behind the scenes. I felt my workforce should know almost everything I knew. The only caveat was when it came to personnel issues. What happens with an employee behind closed doors is private and confidential.

5. Not Making Time for Employees

As a role model and mentor, you need to be approachable and keep your door open for questions, comments, ideas and concerns from your workforce. One of the best practices you can develop is to schedule one-on-one time with the members of your team on a regular basis. This is a valuable tool to assist them in staying focused, inspired and motivated.

4. Not Developing a Vision

If I ask you to think about your home, you don't see the letters *H-O-M-E,* you see a picture of your home. We are wired to think in pictures. Images help us in thinking, understanding and developing plans. In the absence of a vision, what will you picture? That's why a vision statement should be front and center in every organization.

Many organizations have vision statements, but often employees have no idea when theirs says. If you as the leader don't know what your organization's vision is and how it's articulated, how do you reach organizational goals? Moreover, why should employees know and work toward reaching that vision?

Take the opportunity to dust off your vision statement, bring it front and center into the workforce, and outline how each employee's or department's work fits into making that vision a reality. This will allow everyone to have a clear picture of the vision and how they can help reach ultimate success.

3. TAKING IT ALL TOO SERIOUSLY

Leading with your ego only leads to developing an unsuccessful organization. No one wants to work for a tyrant or deal with someone who thinks more about themselves than their workforce. This is something lots of employees deal with daily.

Why did you become a leader? Was it to be able to wear a shirt and tie? To get that parking spot close to the door? Only to make more money? If you said yes to any of these questions, you should really reconsider your commitment to your workforce. Being a leader has nothing to do with you or what it does for you. Being a leader is all about your workforce and making them successful.

What do you see as the measurement of a good leader? Is it the ability to give a presentation? To prepare a line-item budget? Maybe you can work a schedule like nobody's business? That's more management than leadership. As a leader your responsibility is to serve the members of your team. Help them grow, polish skills and become successful. The true measurement of leadership success is strong employee satisfaction, having a highly-engaged workforce and how they ensure an excellent client or customer experience. This cannot happen if you are leading from a "position of authority" mentality. Your ego has no place in the workforce.

Now, there's a fine line between being egotistical and having confidence in your abilities. As a paramedic, my goal was to work hard to be the best I could be. I read constantly, researched medical conditions and their treatments, and began to write and speak on various clinical topics. It was a surprise when my peers labeled me egotistical. This was very confusing to me—until I heard myself rattling off medical jargon and research, sounding like I thought I was better than the folks I was talking to. This made me stop in my tracks and spend time reflecting. Maybe I was coming across as egotistical, not confident. Just because you're good or maybe great at what you do doesn't mean you should flaunt it like a four-carat diamond. Instead focus your knowledge, skills and experience on helping others achieve the same.

2. RESISTING CHANGE

Change is one of those scary, nasty words that's not well received in the business world. Unfortunately one of the keys to being a successful leader is being able to facilitate change. There are always members of the workforce who resist change, but when that person is the leader, that ultimately leads to an organization of status quo and complacency.

"Why do we do it that way?" You hear the same answer all the time; say it with me: "That's the way we've always done it!" An old saying tells you not to fix what's not broken, but just because it's not broken doesn't mean it's efficient or a best practice. Instead develop a standard of challenging your processes. Every so often look at what you're doing and determine if it's the best it can be.

Change is inevitable in organizations, and as a leader you need to know the finer points of how to accept, embrace and facilitate change as business practice dictates. Here are some of the fundamental reasons leaders resist or fear change:

1. Loss of job security;

2. Fear of the unknown;

3. Politics within the organization;

4. Fear of failure;

5. It's not the right time;

6. Not wanting to upset the workforce;

7. Protecting the interests of the group;

8. Lack of employee confidence in the leader's ability to manage change.

These reasons are just excuses people give themselves to stay comfortable. Change is uncertain, uncomfortable and a crapshoot. Sometimes change looks good on paper, then falls flat when it comes to execution.

Be a leader who embraces change. Develop a culture that you're going to work to the best of your abilities and set the standard for others to follow.

1. Failing to Communicate

You should not be surprised to see that failing to communicate is the No. 1 mistake leaders make. We covered communication in Chapter Three. Just remember the importance of being a leader who communicates on a regular basis. Communication promotes motivation, provides the workforce needed information, helps develop positive attitudes and assists in controlling processes.

How to Listen to Your Employees

Listen to your employees. If your employees feel you're not listening, they won't come to you with feedback, suggestions or even status reports. Employees are a company's most valuable assets. They're in the trenches every day, and you need their input to best serve your customers. Even if you're not naturally a good listener, you can become one. Listening isn't a talent you're born with, it's one you develop.

1. **Don't be distracted**—No matter where you are, focus on the person you're talking to. If you allow yourself to be distracted, you may miss an important point and end up spending more time solving a resulting problem than if you'd simply listened carefully from the start. Even if you're listening to someone over the phone and they can't see you, don't check your e-mail or clean out the drawers in your desk.

2. **Don't interrupt**—Don't complete someone else's sentences and don't jump in the minute he or she takes a breath. The speaker should feel like he or she can pause without losing the floor.

3. **Give nonverbal feedback**—Nod your head at appropriate times. Say something here and there. Have an animated expression. Make eye contact.

4. **Don't assume**—You may think you know what someone is about to say—there's a good chance you don't. Keep an open mind and don't try to second-guess. If you don't understand what the person is saying, ask questions or paraphrase what you heard and ask for clarification.

5. **Think before you respond**—Don't jump in the minute the person stops talking. Really think about what he or she said and choose your words carefully.

Active listening is a critical management skill. You can train managers in listening skills, but if the manager believes listening is a way to demonstrate he or she values people, training is usually unnecessary. Listening is providing recognition and demonstrating your values in action. When employees feel heard and listened to, they feel important and respected. You will have much more information when you open the floodgates daily.

You Will Make Mistakes

As a leader you will make mistakes, and that is just something you will need to embrace and understand. I can recall sharing with my workforce a direction the organization was going to head. This direction was a radical move for us. At the end of my talk I remember saying, "Is it going to work? I don't know, but we're going to give it a try." Well, it did not work, and I had to admit so to the workforce. But such is life, and such is leadership. Leaders make mistakes too—it shows you're trying.

CHAPTER EIGHT

Motivate and Inspire to Engage and Satisfy

"The main ingredient of stardom is the rest of the team."

—John Wooden

T he million-dollar question is this: As leaders, what is the best way to motivate and inspire your workforce? Even more important, as a leader, how do you keep yourself motivated and inspired? The opportunity to develop into a leader who achieves ultimate success personally and professionally lies in the ability to answer these two questions.

The strong action of leadership is what makes the difference in motivating employees. Think about the step of motivating as a coach would approach leading his team. We have said it in this book a couple of times: Your job as a leader is to get the very best out of your workforce, and this is no different than manager Joe Torre getting the best out of his 1998 New York Yankees team.

This was the Yankees 96th professional season, and the team finished with a division-winning regular-season record of 114-48. Their closest competitor was the Boston Red Sox, who finished a mere 22 games behind. In the end the Yankees beat the San Diego Padres to capture their 24th World Series title and finished with a combined record of 125 wins and 50 losses, a major-league record.

In a 1998 *New York Times* interview, player Chili Davis said this about Torre: "He's the epitome of what a manager should be. It's not about making moves, or running out there and being noticed, or saying I did this or did that. He took 25 players and, whatever he said to us, he made us all want to go out and bust our butts for him.

To me, when you're going to manage a major-league team, that's the key. You got to have 25 players who want to die for you. That's exactly what Joe did."

What is the recipe that will allow you to motivate your workforce and have them "bust their butts" to become the very best they can? Let's look at the practice of motivating and inspiring your workforce.

MOTIVATION DEFINED

Motivation is the reason or reasons one has for acting or behaving in a certain way. All processes that direct, begin, provide goal-oriented behavior and cause us to act come from motivation. Motivation involves natural, emotional, social and perceptive forces that make specific behaviors possible. These behaviors can be displayed in positive or negative habits.

ELEMENTS OF MOTIVATION

In the 1937 book *Think and Grow Rich,* author Napoleon Hill shares that desire is the starting point of all achievement. He goes on to say that "no one is ready for a thing until he can acquire it." Anyone who has a goal feels the desire, but that desire is not enough to make that goal a reality. There are three elements that will allow your desires to become achievements: activation, persistence and intensity.

1. **Activation**—This is the decision to start an action or behavior.

2. **Persistence**—This is the ability to continue along a chosen path toward reaching your goal regardless of the obstacles or hurdles experienced.

3. **Intensity**—This is the fire that burns inside you for making your goal a reality. It goes hand in hand with persistence. Many times when individuals come across adversity or hit a roadblock or two, it snuffs out their fire, stifling their intensity.

Successful achievement of a goal requires focus, pushing through roadblocks and moving to the next step despite the difficulties.

THEORIES OF MOTIVATION

There are several theories psychologists have proposed to explain motivation. Let's list some below.

1. People are motivated by instinct—Your instincts are natural and fixed behavior patterns driven by basic human needs that stimulate or motivate behavior.

2. Our needs and drives—We have needs for food, hydration and safety. These drives are motivated by our biology. As our body becomes dehydrated, we drink; when we are tired, we sleep. Our needs and drives motivate responses.

3. Arousal levels—One interesting theory suggests individuals engage in behaviors that keep them at an optimum level of arousal. This can include relaxation or thrill-seeking activities.

4. Temporal motivation theory (TMT)—How do deadlines affect motivation levels? This theory deals with the time factor and how it motivates. As a deadline looms closer, it brings a feeling of urgency and importance to complete the task.

5. Incentive theory of motivation—This theory offers that internal (intrinsic) and external (extrinsic) influences motivate human behavior. When a behavior is intrinsic, it sparks individual approval. Intrinsic motivation occurs when an individual finds pleasure and satisfaction in completing a specific task. Extrinsic factors are expected rewards or negative consequences. Examples would be money, praise or fear of corrective action for poor performance.

THE IMPORTANCE OF MOTIVATION

Personal and professional success hinges on motivation. For organizational success, it is those human resources that are the most expensive (as well as the most untapped) that lead to leadership success. When you look at the cultures of successful people and organizations, a common thread is the amount of individual motivation. A workforce that is motivated is engaged. When it's engaged, it's productive, and when a workforce is productive, it gives clients and customers an excellent experience.

Before we discuss the importance of motivation, an important thing to understand is that motivation is a personal attribute. It occurs from either internal or external influences. Due to this fact, leaders cannot motivate anyone. It is the individual who must use sources of motivation to inspire himself. What leaders need to do is create an environment where there are no hurdles for the workforce to become and stay motivated in their daily responsibilities. This realization brings the potential for self-motivation to occur effortlessly.

THE HARDEST TASK

Becoming self-motivated is the hardest task to overcome to achieve ultimate success as a leader. As we mentioned above, motivation occurs from both internal and external sources. As you set off to develop an environment where motivation flourishes, it starts with your self-motivation ability. But at times there are obstacles that sabotage your self-motivation:

1. **Procrastination and excuses**—It's human nature to want to avoid difficult or less-desirable tasks and responsibilities. Looking for distractions and making excuses is the No. 1 characteristic that deflates motivation. Remember back in Chapter Two where we discussed the subconscious mind? When procrastination and excuses occur, the subconscious mind is stirring your need to fail. It is up to you to retrain your subconscious mind to be more positive and not let that negative self-talk derail you. Another factor that explains how procrastination occurs comes from the field of behavioral psychology and is called *time inconsistency.* Even though there are things you want to accomplish—losing weight, getting in shape—time inconsistency is the brain's predisposition to want immediate reward more than future reward. When setting goals for yourself, you are looking toward what your future self will become. Long-term goals set a vision of whom you're looking to develop into. Nevertheless, though you set goals for your future self, your present self is the one

that needs to act to achieve them. Decisions are made in the now. Your present self wants the immediate fulfilment, not the long-term reward. Keep your eye on the prize, stay focused, be persistent and allow your vision to become reality.

2. **The blame game**—The reality is that bad and unexpected things happen. When they do, it's human nature to want to assign blame. When I worked as a paramedic, our life blood was a nice cup of joe (OK, multiple cups). One day my partner and I started our shift with our ritual morning visit to our favorite coffee shop. As we set off to our first posting assignment, I took the top off my coffee to add some ice. A car in front of us forced my partner to hit the brakes with some robustness, and that hot coffee became part of my white shirt. Of course I snapped at my partner, and the driver of the other car may have gotten a snarl. Later my partner said to me, "Guess you'll think twice about taking the top off your coffee in a moving ambulance." He was right, even though I wanted it to be his fault. I was to blame for my own foolishness. Even though blame is a great self-defense mechanism when you're not as perfect as you hoped, blaming others hurts all involved.

Blame is also used as a weapon against those we want to attack. It is easier to throw others under the bus than accept responsibility for our own actions. When this occurs, everyone knows you're passing blame. This works against you on many fronts. You are better off fixing the problem than pointing fingers.

3. **Negative people**—Folks who are always negative suck the life right out of us. I had a friend who was that way—regardless of what happened, there was always fault, blame and condemnation. This behavior eventually caused him to lose all his friends. It was my goal to stick beside him and show him what a real friend was. Regardless of how he acted, what he said, how he treated people, I stayed right there. I can share that eventually it was too much to endure, and that harmful behavior took its toll on my ability to stay positive when I was around him. It was easier for me to conform to being negative in his presence than to change him with positivity. I consider this a failed effort and learned that any future negative people

just need to be let go. Don't allow those people in your life the power to affect your vision, goals, drive or motivation. What you think you become, and if you think negatively or allow negative people to influence you, you become disrupted.

4. **Being standoffish**—Another way leaders protect themselves is by keeping to themselves and not letting people close or accepting help when it's offered. When you're a leader, it's vital to your success to be an influence on everyone. That means projecting a professional and friendly demeanor. It may be easy to keep to yourself and not let anyone in, but to be a successful leader you need to be that go-to person that everyone wants to be around and feels better about themselves when they are.

5. **Not following a plan for success**—What is your plan for success? I know you have one—a vision of your future self, goals to reach that vision and plans to make those goals a reality. One of the failure of leaders is having no plan for growth, development or improving their leadership skills. Remember, what got you in the door won't keep you in the room. It is crucial for your success to become better than you are today. Develop that vision and move yourself forward. Become a leader who invests in growth and never stop your climb toward ultimate success.

6. **The same olé' routine**—One of the most common challenges leaders have is feeling like they're in a rut and not able to grow. As a young paramedic I wanted more—I wanted greatness, the next big success. But every day it was the same olé' routine, the same habits, my same humdrum, mundane day. The secret came when a mentor shared with me to look for my greatness outside my daily habits. She told me, "The reason you can't find the next big thing in your everyday habits is because it's not there. If it were, you would have found it already." Once I understood that, it was amazing on how opportunities came my way. There is a great quote by Les Brown that says, "In order to do something you've never done, you've got to become someone you've never been. I think that all of us have

great potential within us, but greatness is a choice; it's not our destiny. And in the pursuit of our dreams we are introduced to trials, failures and disappointments, which take us to the door of discovery and greatness."

TIPS TO STAY MOTIVATED

Now that we've covered some foundational information on motivation, let's get down to brass tacks and discuss some tips on how to stay motivated:

1. Develop self-awareness—When I'm asked what the most important attribute of leadership success is, my answer is to always develop a high level of self-awareness. You may have good communication skills and be able to resolve conflict, but if you're not sure who you are as a leader or why you react to situations the way you do, it makes no difference how well you can communicate. Take the time to look at yourself as a person, professional and leader. Spend time regularly reflecting on who you are, how you conduct your business, how you handled situations and your leadership style. Reflection and self-awareness are valuable to understanding what motivates you.

2. Pledge yourself to distinction—Excellence and continued development in your career should be what you strive for daily. After you've spent some time reflecting and becoming self-aware, set a vision and plan to develop into the best professional you can be. Once you have that vision, create a guarantee that you will commit yourself to personal excellence. We're in the workforce a long time, and if you must work every day, pledge to doing it with distinction. You will not only feel great about yourself, but you will also inspire those around you. It makes no difference how your day flows; this commitment should never be abandoned. This is something you're doing for you.

3. What are your strengths?—Are you one of those people who beats yourself up for days when mistakes happen? In my

younger days I would kick my own ass for days on end. You must eventually understand that this is an attack against your confidence and self-esteem. Mistakes are part of the learning process that assists us in gaining experience. In my book *Ultimate Leadership: 10 Rules for Success,* rule No. 7 is that experience comes from mistakes, and mistakes come from lack of experience. Name one thing you ever tried that you mastered the very first time! It is a process to develop excellence. This is where knowing your strengths becomes a tool toward your success. As you begin a task, determine what skills are needed for your ultimate success. Knowing your strengths will give you a blueprint to determine if you have the needed skills to be successful. If the answer is yes, you're set. If the answer is no, this may be the time to develop the skills or knowledge to be successful. It is this exercise that will allow you to be prepared for excellence.

4. Be persistent—Think about this question for a minute: Who can stop you from being successful? Is it a peer, maybe your spouse, friends—who? The answer is simple: You are the only one who can keep you from being successful and reaching your goals. Others may have the power to derail you, but you're the only one who decides if that derailment is temporary or permanent. It is paramount that you see yourself as a force. Set your vision of what success looks like for you. See yourself already being successful, and then press full steam ahead toward that vision. If you know you're the only one who can stop you, what's stopping you?

5. Pat yourself on the back—You read that correctly. Why should you only accept the beatings you give yourself when mistakes happen or you fail? In my travels as a coach, I've seen some serious ass kickings from people who continually beat themselves up for mistakes. In full disclosure, I was this person too. When I would make a mistake or forget something while delivering patient care, I'd let that hang around my neck like a hubcap tied to a chain. My mood would be foul; I'd stop talking and question my knowledge. As a result my self-confidence would dip. As a further result, my patient

care would not be up to par for the next couple days, and my motivation would decline for the same period. This was some very damaging behavior on my part. It really took its toll until I found the power of reflection and could grow from my failures.

With that said, with the same vigor with which you beat yourself up, you need to find the satisfaction in a job well done. Take some time each evening to reflect on your successes and reward yourself. Recognize your achievements, no matter how minor, and set out to build on that success the next day. This habit will benefit your confidence and self-image. That will stoke your self-motivation and foster a drive for racking up more successes.

STAYING MOTIVATED DURING STRUGGLE

There will be times when no matter what you do, problems just keep popping up and affecting your day. When these challenging days happen, it is essential that you keep the fire of self-motivation burning strong. That's easier said than done, but developing this habit will eventually grow it into a practice that allows you to stay focused and keep moving on to the next task. Here are some tips to stay focused during challenging times:

1. Stay accountable to yourself—As a leader it is your goal to keep your workforce accountable. With that said, you must also keep yourself accountable to your responsibilities, your workforce and your peers. As a resource, always keep yourself able to deliver on any requests from those who trust your leadership.

2. Stop those negative thoughts—This may be one of the best ways to keep forging forward. As those negative thoughts enter your self-talk, reflect on why what's happening is happening to you, and replace the negative with positive thoughts. Remember, those negative thoughts are coming from the imprinted beliefs of your subconscious mind.

3. Focus on the result—What is the benefit of what you're trying to accomplish? Balance your commitment to your future self against your present self. This will energize you in the tough times.

4. Share your passion—Your passion and positive energy are contagious to those around you. Your workforce looks to you to set the standards of behavior you're expecting. Model the way always and keep your passion front and center.

5. Involve your peers—You have a network for a reason. Rely on those close to you as a resource, sounding board or for advice. Many of those you trust have experienced similar tough times and learning their secrets can assist you in developing a different understanding of the situation.

6. Keep your vision front and center—You should have a personal vision statement outlining where you're heading. Once you get there, whom will you become? What goals do you have for yourself? These are all things that should be captured in your personal vision statement. Once you have that statement, put it where you can see and refer to it in tough times.

When I was in the U.S. Air Force, I was working full time, trying to be the best spouse and parent possible, and going to college full time. For a 25-year-old it was very challenging to keep so many commitments. At times it seemed easier to quit. I sought the counsel of my chief master sergeant, a man who seemed to have all the answers. I shared my thoughts about wanting to quit school, and he asked me why I was taking classes. My response came quickly: "I want to eventually become commissioned as an officer." The chief said to me, "If that's what you want to do, then you have to do everything you can to make that vision a reality." When he told me that, my thought was, *Easier said than done, Chief.* But what he said next was very impactful: "Picture yourself completing college and already wearing those lieutenant bars."

On my way home that evening, I stopped by the military clothing store and bought a set of lieutenant bars and officer collar brass. Once home, I took an old service jacket and placed the bars and brass on it. After that, when things would get tough, even challenging, and thoughts of quitting entered my mind, I would go into my closet and put that service coat on and stand in front of the mirror. That vision gave me the strength to continue and make my dream a reality. It was very motivating to me in tough times.

Keep your vision front and center and remember what you're working toward.

7. Keep a journal—It may sound silly, but instead of keeping your thoughts bottled up, develop the habit of writing them out, reflecting on your notes and determining that way how you can move forward. When I started to record my thoughts, my self-reflection become easier and more rewarding.

To develop ultimate success as a leader, you need to learn how to motivate and inspire. People need to know that when they're around you, you galvanize them and give them a great feeling about themselves. When you learn the power of how to motivate your workforce, step back and watch your department or organization flourish.

CHAPTER NINE
You Are the Visual Aid

"Take advantage of every opportunity to practice your communication skills so that when important occasions arise, you will have the gift, the style, the sharpness, the clarity and the emotions to affect other people."

—Jim Rohn

One of the most important tools for gaining ultimate success as a leader is your ability to communicate. Being able to give direction, coach or have your workforce buy into your vision is what motivates and inspires the necessary people to accomplish a shared goal together. Everything a leader does, says and attains is closely watched by their workforce, peers and clients/customers. My good friend Don Lundy has a saying: "When you leave the house, you step onto the stage, and it's Act 1, Scene 1, and *action*!" For this reason it's vital for your success to be aware of everything you do.

Being able to get your point across in different settings is a valuable skill that needs to be continually mastered. Whether you're speaking one on one, in a staff meeting, in an overview to the board of directors or in front of 5,000 people, the way you communicate is scrutinized from beginning to end. Therefore, you need to cultivate your aptitude for directing, informing, entertaining and persuading whenever possible. In this chapter we focus on the art and science of polishing your public speaking skills.

COMMUNICATION: THE CRUCIAL SKILL

It's not fair by any means, but leaders are often evaluated by their ability to speak effectively and efficiently. I have coached many great leaders who have shared one big challenge: an inability to speak well in public. You may be one of those people, and I can share that there is hope for shifting this challenge into a strength.

One of the secrets is understanding the science of public speaking. From there you begin to develop your speaking style. Once you've developed an effective speaking style, you transform your style into an art. This is what I like to label a "muscle skill"—that is, a skill that gets bigger and stronger every time you use it, and you already know you'll be using it daily.

COMMUNICATION DEFINED

Communication is the sharing of information and ideas with others. This occurs in many different forms: speaking, writing and (most important) nonverbally. For effective communication to take place, there must be four important elements:

1. **The communicator or sender**—The person who has ideas or information to share;

2. **The message**—What the communicator hopes to convey;

3. **The receiver**—The person or group for whom the message is intended;

4. **Feedback**—This element allows the communicator to know the message was received as intended. This is one of the most important parts of the communication process and the one most often overlooked.

FOCUS YOUR COMMUNICATION

My speaker training occurred as a member of the U.S. Air Force. Instructor school was six weeks long and covered every possible nuance of developing into an outstanding "platform instructor." It was here I learned the difference between extemporaneous and impromptu speaking, different questioning techniques and how to analyze your audience.

Once of the biggest lessons was to understand how communication failure happens. This is where I learned to FOCUS my communication skills. *FOCUS* is an acronym that outlines the five principles of good communication. Forgetting or missing the mark with one of these five principles will definitely cause a breakdown in communication. FOCUS stands for *focused, organized, clear, understanding* and *supported.* Let's define each element:

1. **Focused**—The person communicating must make a concentrated effort to present well-defined ideas, objectives and messages to those receiving their communication. When communication is not focused, there can be failure in receiving the appropriate message or responding appropriately.

2. **Organized**—Being organized allows the speaker to take a systematic and logical approach to delivering their message. When delivering a sound message, this will allow the audience to understand without misinterpretation. When preparing to share your thoughts and ideas, take the time to arrange and encode messages properly for maximum comprehension.

3. **Clear**—When you are ready to deliver your message, it is paramount to present the information in clear, concise language. It is a vital component to communication to use proper pronunciation and sentence structure and forego jargon. When we speak in front of people, they are quick to pass judgement for any distorted or incorrect language. This will cause credibility issues and limit acceptance of your message.

4. **Understanding**—This does not cover the understanding of the receiver, but rather your understanding of the receiver's knowledge, level of understanding and how you will deliver the message. If you are delivering your message above the receiver's knowledge level, miscommunication is sure to occur.

5. **Supported**—In the days of the Internet, we see mountains of misinformation taken as fact. When delivering a presentation

or writing a letter, it is vital that you research and include supported information to justify your position. When you share an unsupported message, your credibility comes into question. As you continually try to influence those around you, your views must be trusted.

PREPARING YOUR TALK

When looking to open a successful business, as the old saying goes, it's about location, location, location. When planning to give a presentation, we modify that old saying: Giving an outstanding presentation is about preparation, preparation, preparation. There are 10 steps you'll need to follow if you want to develop a successful presentation.

If you were thinking about building a house, you wouldn't just set off one morning and begin to build. You would follow a blueprint that outlines the steps to completing a successful project. If you follow these 10 steps, this will act as your blueprint for success. One of the biggest fears is speaking in front of people. That fear can be reduced considerably when you know the exact steps your presentation takes.

YOUR 10-STEP BLUEPRINT

1. Know Your Audience

This is where you determine the purpose of the presentation and to whom you will be speaking. Recently I was contacted by an organization that wanted me to speak at their event. This talk would be for approximately 1,000 attendees. When I received the e-mail, the direction was, "We are looking for some motivational leadership topics." That seemed like a very broad brush to begin a fine painting. I set up a time to talk to the organizer and asked the following questions:

- What is the purpose of the gathering? Is this a convention? Sales meeting? Or maybe a celebration? Understanding why these folks are gathered will allow you to focus on why they're in the same room together. In this case it was the kickoff for a big sales campaign for the rest of the year.

- What positions do the individuals hold within the organization? This is a very important step in developing the presentation and determining a level of engagement. Ensure the talk will meet the audience's level of expectation.

As a paramedic, one of my favorite topics to teach was cardiology. I love talking about the heart—its anatomy, physiology and functions. As part of my teaching experience, I had the opportunity to present this topic to many different allied healthcare professionals, paramedic students and even cardiologists. Even though the information was technically the same, for each presentation it was essential the information given was tailored for the audience's fundamental comprehension. So I would ask myself: In what format would they like the material presented? Is this a discussion? A formal presentation? Are they expecting a PowerPoint? Will there be a Q&A session? What is the time limit?

Such questions will allow you to understand the parameters of how the lecture will be delivered. They will also give you the ability to do some self-reflection. If you're being asked to give a formal lecture to 1,000 individuals, are you comfortable in that space? If you only have experience speaking to 50 people in an informal discussion, are you prepared to handle this bigger audience? Another factor is ensuring you're knowledgeable with the material you're asked to speak about.

MEETINGS THE AUDIENCE'S EXPECTATIONS

Meeting the expectations of the audience is your fundamental goal when speaking. Here are a few tips when to make certain you have success with your audience.

- **Don't be intimated by who is in the room**—I've known speakers who have gotten disrupted because the CEO unexpectedly entered the room or the president of the hospital system joined the audience. You have done your research, prepared your information and were ready to present before the president showed up. Just continue along as planned and give them the best performance possible.

- **Be respectful**—When leading a presentation, always remember the golden rule: Treat others as you'd like to be treated. Never use your position as a presenter to embarrass or "one up" someone in your audience.

- **Be all-encompassing**—As you analyze your audience, it is crucial to remember it will include a diverse group of individuals. Adhere to good taste and ensure you do not alienate a specific group of people.

- **Spread the energy**—Let them feel your passion. If you're not passionate about what you're presenting, why should the audience be passionate to learn what you have to say? Let them feel your energy and make it contagious.

2. Do Your Homework

Now that you know whom your audience is going to be, it becomes time to develop your topic to meet their needs. There are several lectures in my speaker's toolbox. Some of my favorites have been used, polished and redefined for many years. Regardless of how many times I've presented a specific topic, my preparation is always the same. It always includes breaking down the outline and ensuring it flows correctly, the material is fresh and it will meet the expectations of the audience. Here are some things to focus on when researching your topic.

- **Know your timeline**—Don't let time get away from you when preparing for your talk. As a professional speaker, folks will engage with me up to six months in advance of their event. Once the agreement is made, I outline on my calendar when my preparation should begin and finish. It may be easy to keep saying, "I have time" or "Next week, next week." When you keep putting off researching your topic, you only add to the stress, apprehension and uneasiness that lead to nervousness. Know your timeline and set concrete deadlines for research.

- **Rely on your mentors**—Let's say you're presenting on increasing employee satisfaction. Speaking to and maybe even interviewing your mentors and members of your professional network can bring in a wealth of information and perspectives. This is a great way to engage new ideas, practices and differences of opinions. I have even said in a presentation, "A colleague of mine believes *x;* this differs from my view, but I want to share how others see this issue."

- **Remove biases**—In giving a presentation, make certain you're not injecting your personal views. When researching, use a mode that will allow you to keep personal values and beliefs out of the discussion.

- **Use Google**—Wow, there is a wealth of information on the Internet. Be careful when researching your topic, though. Although there may be much information available, that doesn't necessarily mean it's truthful. If a source provides a specific point you'd like to use, try to verify it from at least two more sources before you repeat it as fact.

3. Back Up Your Main Points

Once you've researched your topic and know the main points you'll be presenting, it is vital that your main points are backed up and supported as you work through your presentation. As you go through your research, bring supportive information into your presentation as needed.

4. Develop Your Outline

In the age of PowerPoint, speakers have gotten out of the habit of developing outlines for their presentations. Simply put, your outline is your blueprint to delivering an exceptional performance. If you are a speaker who likes to use PowerPoint, it's practical to develop your outline first, then move to creating supporting slides.

Set up outlines that allow you to present your topic in a systematic and logical way. Let's say you're developing a presentation on basic leadership skills. Your audience will be a group of 50 newly promoted supervisors. You will have 90 minutes for your lecture. Your knowledge gives you the ability to talk to this group.

Now that you have the foundational information about your audience, your research of the topic begins. What are the objectives you'd want to share with new supervisors to help them become successful in their new positions?

When developing your outline use the following template:

- **Attention step**—This is where you gain the audience's attention. Think about any class you've attended. Prior to the speaker beginning their talk, what was going on in the room? Were individuals talking? Was the room loud or quiet? Were people standing and shaking hands? The attention step is just that: a way to get the audience's attention. You can begin with a quote, a statistic or two, maybe even a story. In the case of this presentation, an example would be: "According to Gallup only 29% of your workforce is highly engaged, 54% is disengaged, and 17% is actively disengaged. How can you be successful with almost three-quarters of your workforce either disengaged or actively disengaged?"

- **Motivation step**—Your motivation step is about explaining to the audience why this presentation is important to them. In developing this presentation, you spent a great deal of time getting to know your audience. As you developed this knowledge, you should have outlined why your information has significance to them. The motivation step gives the audience a clear understanding of what this class means to them. Adding to the attention step, here is a great transitional motivation step: "How do you measure a leader's success? Is it the ability to prepare a line-item budget? Maybe how creative you are in managing a schedule? Perhaps your success as a leader is based on how well you develop your professional network? No, really it's none of these things. The true measure of a leader's success is how satisfied they are at work. When they are satisfied they become highly engaged. A highly engaged workforce yields increased productivity and makes certain your clients and customers have an excellent experience. When all those things occur, that outlines your success as a leader. But how can you achieve leadership success if only 29% of your workforce is highly engaged? Over the next 90 minutes, we are going to outline the skills you need to develop a highly engaged workforce."

Introduce yourself. You have their attention, and you've outlined why the class is important. Now you must establish your credibility. Why should you be the person to listen to? True, all the things you mentioned above are important, but why are you the person the audience needs to guide them?

This is where you get into the crux of delivering your information, the body of your talk. Use a main point/subpoint format. An example would be:

MAIN POINT #1: LEADERSHIP STYLES

SUBPOINT #1: DISCUSS THE IMPORTANCE OF DEVELOPING A STRONG LEADERSHIP STYLE.

SUBPOINT #2: EXPLAIN THE FIVE MAIN LEADERSHIP STYLES:

a. Autocratic;
b. Participative;
c. Transactional;
d. Transformational;
e. Laissez-faire.

SUBPOINT #3: OUTLINE THE CONCEPT OF SERVANT LEADERSHIP.

Then complete your presentation in the same manner, listing main points with supportive subpoints. The number of main points will depend on how much time you have and how much information you'd like to share.

- **Summary**—Once you've completed the body of your presentation, it's time to begin your summary. Your summary is where you give a compact version of your talk. Highlight and overview the main points, and share some supportive facts. This is your last chance to drive home why this information is important to your listeners' success. An example would be: "We have covered some good and valuable information here today. Remember, the success of a leader depends on how strongly your workforce is committed to their duties and responsibilities and how engaged they are in the success of the organization. A year from now, what will your leadership autobiography say about you? Will you have an engaged workforce, or will you be playing catchup with your disengaged members? Ladies and gentlemen, apply the information we talked about today and continue to write the next chapter in your leadership success."

- **Closing**—This is where you end your presentation. Be humble and show gratitude for being able to visit with the audience.

5. Obtain Feedback

Once you feel comfortable you have an outline that will exceed expectations, it's a best practice to share your outline with a mentor, peer or someone who has solid speaking experience.

Talk through each component of your outline, overview your audience and share what your research has shown. Use this step also to gain the other person's perspective on how they would present the material. Ask questions and make tweaks as necessary. Remember, your outline should be a living document; as things pop up, you should make changes as necessary. Another great resource that comes from sharing your outline with others is that you get to hear the stories and experiences of those individuals.

In preparing for a recent talk, I visited with a peer and shared an overview of an upcoming presentation. The discussion was going to revolve around managers who led with their ego, were selfish or had a disregard for their workforce. As we discussed my approach to my presentation, he shared a story of a leader who'd taken over his previous position after my friend had taken a new one. My friend was a servant leader, but his replacement took a me-first approach to leadership. Because of this approach, in less than a year, employee engagement was down, attrition increased by 50% and productivity was dismal. Due to this horrible performance by this selfish leader, he was replaced some 13 months after being given the job. This story was a great example of poor leadership, and I could use it in my presentation to drive some main points home.

6. Preparation

7. Preparation

8. Preparation

This is no misprint; preparation is the single most important factor when it comes to delivering an excellent presentation. Everything done to this point in developing your presentation comes under the heading of preparation, but now it's actually time to recite and act things out. Some best practices here should include:

- Use a video camera, so you can see your movements, gestures and how you look during your presentation. When watching your presentation, take notes and use them to bolster your next practice. Try to allow enough time to video yourself three to four times.

- Use an audio recorder to analyze how your presentation flows. Take notice of your conversational speed, tone, inflection and any vocalized pauses. The continual use of *ahs* and *ums* are killers to presentations.

- Conduct a dress rehearsal. One of the benefits of growing up in New York City was the opportunity to be part of the audience for a few *Saturday Night Live* performances. Being able to walk the halls of the NBC studios was an incredible opportunity. On a couple of occasions, with some inside help, I even got tours of some of the other NBC studios and to see some historic NBC sets. The reason I bring this up is that everyone knows *SNL* comes on at 11:30 p.m. ET every Saturday night. What a lot of folks do not know is that there is a full dress rehearsal at 7 p.m. in front of another live audience. This allows the powers that be to see how skits will work and the laughs they get, and prepare for the live show later that evening.

Taking a page from this historic show, use this best practice to do a dress rehearsal prior to your live show. As I would help members of my workforce prepare for speaking on the big stage, it was part of their preparation to give their presentation to another audience beforehand. This allowed the speaker to see how the audience reacted to their information. This presentation was videotaped and analyzed later for tweaking as needed.

You may be asking yourself how much preparation you should put in prior to giving the final presentation. As a rule of thumb, you should have 4–5 hours of practice for every hour of stage time. This will give you the confidence needed to feel comfortable with the material and understand its flow and how the information will be delivered. This step—or, here, three steps—is the single most important factor in delivering the best presentation possible. In the next section we will cover the finer points of delivery and developing solid presentation skills.

9. Seek Feedback

Once the presentation is over, find a way to get feedback from the audience. Every time I speak there is always a group of individuals who want to ask questions, ask for my card or just say, "Great job." I like to ask these folks what they thought of the presentation with the following questions:

- Did the presentation meet your expectations?
- What part of the presentation resonated with you?
- Was there something I spent too little or too much time on?
- What is the one thing you will take from this presentation and implement in your practice?

If you can have your listeners complete formal evaluations, it's a great tool for polishing and tweaking your presentation for next time. With that said, whenever you have the chance to fill out an instructor evaluation, take a few minutes and give some real solid and truthful feedback. This is a crucial tool for the instructor to hone and polish their skills.

10. Do a Final Assessment

Tons of work went into developing your presentation. Once the date has passed and everything worked as planned, take a moment to reflect and write an overview of everything that happened during this period. These notes will become part of the historical record for this class. You never know, there may be a time you need to dust off this presentation and give it to another audience. It would be great to open your journal and see what succeeded, what needed polish and what would make the presentation work better next time.

PRESENTATION SKILLS

When you stand in front of an audience, it makes no difference if it's 10 people or 5,000, you should consider it a performance. You are putting yourself on public display, and when people have their eyes on you, they're looking at every aspect of your appearance, your movement, your gestures and oh, by the way, what you're saying. For this reason you need to understand the art and science behind how to present your message.

To become effective as a presenter, you need to be adaptable, energetic and allow your enthusiasm to become contagious. It is your presentation skills that take your written presentation and enhance it into a visual, inspirational public performance. In this section we focus on the components that make up your presentation skills and help ensure your delivery is successfully received.

As you set out to deliver the best possible presentation, focus on the following points; your skills will need to grab the audience's attention, inspire their vision and cultivate their understanding.

USING YOUR VOICE

The name of this chapter is "You Are the Visual Aid." One of the most important factors in delivering a presentation is that all eyes are on you. Even if you have a superb PowerPoint with a magnificent handout, *you* are the most important visual aid, and you need to put yourself front and center during your talk.

Your voice is the one thing you can control that will complement your presentation and engage your audience or extinguish your presentation's success. Have you ever listened to a presentation delivered in monotone? Just typing this line makes me yawn at the thought. When attending a presentation, people are looking to be informed, entertained, directed or persuaded. The way you vocalize your message is vital to your success. Here are some tips to deliver a vocally strong presentation:

Verbal construction—When you prepare to speak, focus on three components that are key to effective speaking. They are volume, or making sure you can be heard; clarity, making sure you are understood; and variation, which adds the interest and variety to your talk.

Volume—This is a feature you need to be aware of always. Find a right volume that is appropriate for the room, allows for clear understanding and emphasizes key points that occur throughout your talk. Everyone has their own distinct way of speaking; some have deep, booming voices, while others speak with naturally soft voices and have challenges in projecting it. *Volume* does not mean you should be yelling at the audience. Instead project your voice to the back of the room. If you're not using a microphone, focus your talk on the person farthest from you. Find a level the person in the back can understand but that isn't overbearing. When using a microphone, check your volume by asking the people in the back of the room if they can hear you comfortably. Using your volume is about developing a strong voice, while allowing your breath to become synchronized with your words. The more you use your breath, the farther you will be able to project your voice.

Clarity—Back in 1989 I was giving a talk to some VIPs visiting my Air Force base. A major came to me and said, "Are you clear when you speak?" I must have looked confused, because he laughed and said, "There are a couple of individuals in this group who are deaf and read lips, so good pronunciation, avoiding jargon and keeping your message as clear as possible will help them understand."

I was just 24, and this increased my nervousness tenfold, making me want to throw up a lung. I spoke to one of my supervisors, and his advice was to just do the best job I could. As I look back now on that experience, it taught me the importance of making sure that when speaking, my message was as clear and simple as possible. Some 28 years later, if there is one piece of advice I share most with new speakers, it is this very lesson: When you speak, keep your words simple, don't speak through clenched teeth, and speak naturally.

Variation—They say variety is the spice of life, and this is true when it comes to speaking as well. To make your talk interesting, effective and entertaining, it is vital that you apply the techniques of speaking at a good *pace,* using appropriate *volume,* have good *voice inflection* and use the power of a *pause.*

- **Pace**—Being a native New Yorker, one of my biggest challenges has been how fast I speak. As I get more excited, my pace increases, and my New York accent becomes more pronounced. Your pace of speech is computed by the number of words spoken per minute. A slow pace would be considered fewer than 110 words per minute (wpm), and a conversational pace would be 120 wpm on the low end and between 160–200 on the high end.

- **Volume**—Using the volume of your voice will assist you in creating emphasis.

- **Inflection**—In my opinion, using vocal inflection is one of the most important characteristics of a successful talk. This is where you display energy and enthusiasm for your message. Being able to emphasize words or phrases at specific times drives main points home, shares excitement and makes your passion contagious.

- **Pauses**—The use of pauses is a powerful tool. Use a pause to drive a point home, allow a message to be absorbed and help the listener become more engaged in your point. Your listeners translate meaning during pauses. Also, when you use pauses in this way, it conveys expertise, assurance and sincerity.

  Vocalized pause is the name we give to syllables like "a," "uh," "um" and "ah," often used at the beginning of sentences. While a few vocalized pauses are natural and do not distract, too many impede the communication and learning processes. Avoid overusing stock expressions such as "OK," "like" and "you know." These serve no positive role in communication and only convey a lack of originality.

- **Be dynamic**—To give a presentation is to deliver a performance. You are on stage, all eyes are on you, and you must perform at your very best. Being dynamic, showing enthusiasm and letting your audience feel your passion is an essential component of a successful performance. When it comes to a topic, remember this: There are no boring topics, only boring presenters. When you are dynamic and energetic and display enthusiasm, your audience will be more involved with your message.

    1. *Body movement*—Many speakers I've witnessed over the years seemed to grow roots, standing in the same spot while giving their talks. If not for their mouths moving, they would have looked like statues. Again, you are the visual aid, and every time you speak, all eyes are on you. Your goal is to be dynamic, and one of the most important factors in that is to have good, natural body movement. When you have good body movement, this not only catches the listener's eye but also their attention. Purposeful body movement will also assist with changing your pace, volume and inflection. Another benefit of movement is that it helps burn off that excess energy that comes with being nervous. As you get use to using movement during your talk, you will quickly notice how at ease you become.

    2. *Gestures*—Along with body movement, you must also use gestures to emphasize your talk. These should be purposeful movements of your hands, arms and head to support what you're saying. Wave your arms, use your hands, slip a hand into your pocket—just make sure movements are purposeful and natural. Being Italian, I have heard this joke many times: *How do you stop an Italian from talking? Tie their hands behind their back.* It is not only funny but partially true. As I speak, I feel so uncomfortable if I can't use my hands to make a point, show emphasis or give direction, I'm lost.

       One thing to remember when using your hands is not to fidget—this will distract from your message. I once sat through a 90-minute presentation during which the speaker rattled the change in his pocket for 50 of those minutes. What do I remember about his talk? He was the pocket change guy.

Stage fright—You probably know that stage fright is one of most people's biggest fears. When I tell people I do motivational speaking, they often say they wish they could speak comfortably in front of groups. My response is always the same: There's no reason you can't. Like anything else, public speaking is a skill—a skill that must be mastered for effectiveness.

Over my career I have trained hundreds of people in the art and science of speaking. In one course, as I outlined the contents, expectations and workload, I heard someone from the second row turn to her friend and say, "I think I made a mistake coming here."

During my courses there is one very distinct exercise participants must face on the first day. First we have an initial discussion of why public speaking is so scary. Answers include not knowing what to say, possibly forgetting the material and not being able to ask questions. I want to address this fear almost right away; the exercise is called the "pink box." Inside the pink box are several topics that include things like brushing your teeth, balancing your checkbook, talking yourself out of a speeding ticket and shaving your legs. You must come up, pick a topic and speak about the topic for two minutes. I usually allow the students to put the first topic they draw back if they don't like it, but they must talk on the second one.

Now the kicker: Before the first person comes up, I regularly march 20–30 outsiders into the class to watch the exercise. As soon as this happens, you hear the moans and groans. Even though students hate this exercise, they usually do it well the first time. Once the exercise is complete, the question I always ask is, "What would have made this exercise easier?" The response is always the same: if they knew the topic beforehand.

What is the answer to stage fright? Prepare your talk, know your material and prepare, prepare, prepare. I became an instructor in 1986, and to this day I still have stage fright. To me it's like riding a roller coaster: You do it for the thrill. When you stop being nervous about speaking, it's probably time to stop speaking.

Eye contact—Finally, one of the most important components of speaking is to make appropriate eye contact with those listening to you. This is the most important nonverbal communication skill for success. When you have effective eye contact, three things will happen:

1. It allows you to gauge the listeners' nonverbal feedback. You can see the responses to your statements and points.

2. It lets the listener know you respect and are interested in them.

3. Your delivery, credibility and professionalism are enhanced.

Good eye contact shows you have the sincere desire to connect with your audience, makes it evident you're trying to speak to every person and gains your listeners' esteem.

You may be thinking this chapter seems more geared toward public speaking than group or one-on-one speaking. It's all the same speaking. Develop the skills to speak to a group of 100, and you will also have the skills to speak to a group of two. Learn the science of speaking, and it will become a great love and something you seek to do.

CHAPTER TEN
It's About Correcting the Action

"It's not about the coaching. It's about watching the employee's growth."

—Chris Cebollero

The days of "command and control," or leading from a position of authority, are over. They have been for a very long time, but it seems leaders haven't caught up to that concept. One of the most common leadership mistake I notice when assisting organizations is how leaders approach their workforces.

I've heard leaders say their workers "should just be happy we give them jobs." Then they wonder why they have issues with employee satisfaction and engagement.

In every policy manual I look at, it seems there's always a policy regarding corrective action. Some of these policies are strict and have terms like *zero tolerance, progressive action* and *acceptable standards.* All seem to have the verbal, written, final written and dreaded termination stages of disciplinary action. Some organizations may even have added suspension as an option before termination. One of the biggest failures with the corrective action process is that leaders use this as punishment and forget they're trying to remedy an action or behavior. Leaders need to change their focus from reacting to the symptoms of an issue and instead determine the cause of the problem.

In all stages of my career, I have received some sort of counseling or corrective action. Heck, in my younger years I could have wallpapered my bedroom with all the paper that was written about my performance, or lack thereof. It seems organizations are quick to jump to the corrective action policy, document a verbal warning or give a written reprimand to employees who aren't cutting it. Then, once that corrective action is completed, we label those employees as low performers.

This is a big oversight on the part of our leaders. Those employees you've just counseled need your leadership even more than before. If you're just writing them off, you are truly failing them. If we think about the purpose of the corrective action process, it is not for punishment, but rather to help employees correct an action. Instead leaders use it as a hammer. There is, however, a silver bullet to achieving your ultimate success: You must transform your philosophy from one that relies on punitive action and instead develop the skills to coach employees toward success.

STOP LABELING EMPLOYEES

One failure of leaders is that they are quick to brand employees as subpar, low performers or problem children. This is a natural occurrence when leaders see something they think is out of the ordinary. It occurs secondary to the laws of logic. There are three laws of logic: the law of identity, the law of noncontradiction and the law of the excluded middle. Logic is the foundation of critical thinking and exceptionally useful in determining truth and finding mistakes. But the laws of logic will also cause us to believe things that may not be true about our employees.

1. **The law of identity**—In basic terms this law says something is what it is. A banana is a banana. We know this by its characteristics, and it only has one identity.

2. **The law of noncontradiction**—This law says something cannot be two things at the same time or in the same sense. For the most part people can recognize when someone is contradicting themselves. For example, I tell you I changed the oil in my car yesterday, then later I tell you I did not change the oil in my car yesterday. You would say this is a contradiction, because you know both statements can't be true. The principle of this law is that truth is not self-contradictory.

3. **The law of the excluded middle**—Basically this law says a statement is either true or false. The principle of this law is important because it deals with absolutes. As a male I cannot say I am pregnant; you would know immediately this was not true. So once you name something, it either is or isn't.

This is an important concept as it pertains to leadership; let me explain why. If we take what we learned with the law of the excluded middle, when we label an employee "subpar," we believe the statement to be true. Every time we look at that employee, all we see is a subpar employee. This is a crucial error of leaders that needs to be corrected. In short, labeling people for what they do does not make them who they are.

WHY EMPLOYEES DISPLAY CHALLENGES

Instead of labeling employees when you see something out of the ordinary, spend some time to find out why what you witnessed occurred. Once I witnessed a new employee do something that was against one of our policies. I remember going to the supervisor on duty to share what I saw. I felt it important that the supervisor should address this policy violation. I remember being annoyed that a new employee would do something so flagrant. When the supervisor returned to me, the employee had mentioned that during his orientation, that was how his field training officer had taught him to handle that situation. That was an interesting revelation to me. Until the supervisor reported back, my thoughts focused around having hired the wrong employee, trying to figure out how a new employee had the boldness to not follow policy, and considering cutting our losses at this early stage, as surely this employee would become a low performer.

Once further information revealed this may have been a training issue, I questioned my own failure to be nonbiased, give the employee the benefit of the doubt and know my employees better. Being quick to jump the gun and define an employee based on what I saw was unjust. This failure caused me to reflect on my own way of thinking. It caused me to research and study employee motivation, behavior and behavior modification. As my career progressed, it became apparent to me that when employees had issues or challenges in completing their duties and responsibilities, it was usually due to one of four issues. These are:

1. **Training issues**—The employee was not trained correctly. Shortcuts were taken, or the employee may need some additional training.

2. **Equipment challenges**—The employee is not using or does not have the right equipment, tools or resources to do their job or meet their responsibilities.

3. **Environmental concerns**—Something in the employee's surroundings or work environment is causing a challenge for completing assigned duties and responsibilities.

4. **Behavior problems**—If the above three issues are not a factor, it may in fact just be a behavior issue that requires some coaching, counseling or performance improvement strategies.

The above is only a brief explanation of employee behavior and leadership failure. To become a successful leader, you must spend more time learning, studying and researching all the above to be fair, supportive and nonbiased for your employees.

Now let's turn our discussion to one of the most important skills a leader needs to have for ultimate success, coaching.

COACHING DEFINED

People do not buy services or products; what they buy is outcomes for their needs, desires or problems. As leaders we are worried about schedules, budgets, going to meetings and completing projects. Your front-line supervisors should be focused on supporting the workforce, guiding them, polishing them and helping them grow. This is where coaching needs to become a big part of growing your team. Coaching, simply put, is the process of helping your workforce develop their skills, abilities and competencies for their areas of responsibility. When you coach your workforce, you are working to bring out the very best in them. This is an incredible responsibility and one that will pay off 10 times over.

Why Coach

The true measure of a leader's success is the employee's satisfaction, engagement, productivity and ensuring the client/customer has an excellent experience. We invite members to join our workforce to help our organization become successful. As leaders it is vital to invest all efforts in ensuring your team is motivated, inspired, satisfied and engaged. This is where coaching is a vital link in organizational success. You are the greatest influence over the success or failure of your team. By equipping your workforce with the knowledge, skill and experience that brings them to their next level, you build confidence, self-esteem and loyalty.

Give More Feedback

As we've discussed, leaders are more focused on management than leadership—getting to this meeting, meeting that deadline, completing another project. When responsibilities pull leaders in other directions, their focus on their workforce is minimal. When a problem happens with an employee and we must take time away from what we deem is more important, leaders get, let's say, a bit more bothered. There is nothing more important than ensuring your workforce has everything it needs for success. It is crucial for your success as a leader that you not only find time to give feedback but also meet that commitment on a regular basis. It is this lack of feedback that leads to a lack of performance or hardwiring skills that are not being performed correctly.

Giving feedback needs to be done face to face and with sincerity. For some reason in business, when we try to give constructive or corrective feedback, the response always seems to be defensive. Who really likes to receive constructive feedback? People always say they can take it, but sometimes animosity exists. You need to find the best way to give feedback, corrective or constructive, in the most positive way possible.

Part of the duties of being a paramedic is alerting the hospital of incoming patients being transported. This allows the hospital to give instructions back to the paramedic and prepare the patient care area. This report should be short and sweet, just a snapshot of the patient, their complaint and the treatment given. I had one paramedic—let's call him Sammy—who always gave lengthy reports. His reports were full of useless and irrelevant information. His peers would make fun of him, and even nurses at the area hospitals started reacting negatively.

LET THE COACHING BEGIN

One of the challenges of dealing with professionals in the emergency medical services is ego. These healthcare professionals leave EMS training with a chip on their shoulders. They think they know all the answers, understand all the treatments and can do their jobs better than anyone else. Ego is the biggest barrier to success for an EMT or paramedic. So when it's time to coach, consider the approach and how to help the individual not only see the problem but also find a solution.

COACHING FOR SUCCESS

A coaching with Sammy would look something like this:

Chris Cebollero (CC): Hey, Sammy, how are things going with you today?

Sammy Lunchmeat (SL): Hey, chief, thing are going well, just ran a good call.

CC: Sam, where do you feel your strengths lie as a paramedic?

SL: Well, I love cardiology and trauma calls; I think they make me the most comfortable.

CC: I am a big cardiology fan as well. Now let's flip the coin: What do you feel are the biggest challenges to your success?

SL: Pediatric calls give me some anxiety, as well as my navigation around the city.

CC: Navigation was a challenge for me as well. You know, Sam, I've been listening to a couple of your radio reports to the hospital. How is that skill helping you in your patient care?

SL: I do seem to have some problems with giving the best information sometimes.

CC: What do you feel the challenges to be?

SL: It doesn't seem I have a good flow within my communication.

CC: If you'd like to spend some time with me, maybe we can develop a script where you can just plug in the needed information and be more focused all the time?

SL: That would be great!

CC: Let's chat toward the end of this week. I'll pull some of your radio calls and some other ones for an example, and we'll develop what works best for you.

The thing to notice here: This was not confrontational. It allowed Sam to recognize his own issue, and I offered my help to turn his weakness into a strength. Being a good coach is not about having the best answers; it's about pulling the best answers out of the individual you're helping.

Breaking Down the Barriers

As a leader, you should know first and foremost that you cannot motivate anyone. All motivation comes from the individual's intrinsic or extrinsic motivators. Your fundamental obligation as a leader is to break down the hurdles within your organization to allow for motivation and inspiration to occur.

Barriers to coaching and motivation do not just happen in organizations. Many employees we invite into our teams have their own barriers to becoming successful. As the leader you must determine where the employee's challenges originate.

When children are born, they only have two inherent fears: a fear of falling and a fear of loud noises. As they get older, every other fear is picked up from their parents, friends or experiences. Some of these learned fears are alive and well even today in the business world. There are two fears employees always seem to carry into the workplace that you must help them overcome: the fear of disappointment and the fear of rejection.

1. **Fear of disappointment**—This is also known as fear of failure. It is one of the most self-destructive behaviors we see in the business world. This fear is what keeps individuals inside their comfort zone, never venturing out or exploring professional

development opportunities. Procrastination is prevalent, excuses grow, and poor or nonperformance results.

2. **Fear of rejection**—This also manifests as fear of criticism or contempt resulting from an action. This is another factor that prevents branching out to try something new. If your employee fails, they will be made fun of or dismissed from their clique or group.

As a leader it is paramount that you remove these barriers and create a culture where everyone learns together, mistakes are accepted and a sense of belonging exists. Do not develop into a one-mistake organization. Name one thing you ever mastered the first time you tried! It took time to learn, read and make practical mistakes. Now, as you begin to gain the skill of coaching, you will be able to watch the transformation as your workforce grows.

FACE-TO-FACE COACHING

Before we discuss the outline of a coaching session, it is important to understand that when you coach your employee, your coaching can be based on a positive or negative subject. Just as you would schedule time to discuss a challenge the employee has, take the same time to schedule a meeting for something you saw the employee do correctly or excel at. It is crucial that your workforce knows that when you come to visit with them, it is not because you're just delivering bad news.

As you set up your face-to-face session, consider the following steps:

1. Remove yourself from your office and find a nonthreatening place for this session to take place. This session should be one on one, with every effort made to minimize interruptions.

2. If there is need for a third person to be involved, all communication should be between the leader and the employee. Never engage the third person, as it will look like you are ganging up on the employee.

3. Schedule and allot as much time as needed to conduct a successful coaching session.

4. Create an environment that is nonthreatening and free from negative emotion.

5. Begin your discussion. One of the best ways to allow this to happen is to ask questions to gain an understanding of the situation without causing alarm or leading the employee to become defensive.

ASK MORE QUESTIONS

John Maxwell wrote a great book called *Good Leaders Ask Great Questions.* I remember when reading this work how easy it seemed to elicit information, gain perspective and understand the other point of view by asking questions and not jumping to conclusions.

In the case of developing a coaching development plan for employees, there is a lot of information that needs to be determined before a plan can be created. If you go into a coaching session with a preconceived notion of guilt or an outcome in mind you want to attain, you have already done an injustice to your employee. Remember, the purpose of coaching is not to use punitive action as a tool but rather to gain an understanding of the foundational issue and together develop a plan to make this a strength for the employee.

DOES A PROBLEM EXIST?

This is the first step in determining if coaching needs to take place. Lay the cards out on the table and outline what you as the leader interpret the issue to be. This is a very important word, because what you *interpret* the issue to be may in fact be no issue at all. So outline your thoughts and allow the employee to share their ideas about the situation. Allow for open dialogue to take place for everyone's total foundational understanding of the issue.

Jim was a great employee—he always came to work on time, had a smile on his face and went the extra mile. The trouble with Jim seemed to start when he was passed over for a promotion he thought he was sure to get. What made the situation worse was that the individual who was promoted instead, Julie, worked on Jim's team, and there seemed to be some animosity between them after that. Secondary to that promotion, Jim started to come to work late, leave a bit early and produce subpar work. Since these were unusual traits for him, I wanted to have a chat and get to the bottom of it.

I remember walking up to Jim and asking him how he was doing, if there was anything he needed from me. Without making eye contact, he just smiled and said things were fine. So then I asked Jim to join me for a cup of coffee—I told him I wanted to bounce some ideas off him. As we sat in the break room, I made some small talk, asking about his family and hobbies, then asked the big question: "Jim, I was wanting to get your opinion on Julie being awarded the new position. I know you were both up for it, and I want to know how you perceive the promotion."

Jim just smiled and said nothing. From his lack of response, I knew this was a sore topic for him.

Jim went on to tell me how he felt Julie was not a strong leader— her work skills were only fair, and at times she badmouthed the organization. I asked Jim, "How long has this been going on with your direct report?" He said about five months prior to her promotion. "Looks like we may have dropped the ball here, Jim," I told him.

I then asked Jim if he could go back to his office and get me all the written notices and corresponding paperwork regarding Julie's poor performance so I could consider the issue further. As I suspected, there was no corresponding paperwork to look over.

As we chatted and I dug a bit deeper, I found it really had nothing to do with Julie's work performance. It was more about Jim being passed over for a promotion he thought he deserved.

DEFINE COMMON SOLUTIONS

As the conversation went along, I mentioned some of the things I'd been noticing over the past few weeks: tardiness, subpar work, leaving a bit earlier each day. Then I asked Jim if he noticed the same characteristics. He of course had noticed his heart was not in his work recently.

Very quickly we came to some common ground that needed to be addressed. I asked Jim, "Are you still wanting to be a member of our organization?" He did not answer right away and just looked at the ground. He then replied that he did wish to continue to work for the organization. We now needed to come up with a defined coaching plan that would allow Jim to become more productive and me to assist his transition back.

CHOOSE APPROPRIATE SOLUTIONS

After reaching common ground, it was now time we outlined appropriate solutions that would allow Jim to get back on track. He committed to arriving at work 15 minutes before his start time; asking his peers to check over his work; and stopping leaving early. As part of this solution, I also offered to meet with Jim once a month for an hour to go over his personal vision, goals and plans for his future. This would allow me to act as a mentor to get him to the next level in his career. In addition, if Jim needed anything beyond our monthly meetings, he could pop in and get those items addressed. From my side, I wanted to make certain that I stopped by his work area periodically and gave him words of encouragement and motivation.

One of the things you must remember is that once people feel they are a problem within the organization, they feel lost, anxious or that they are soon to be fired. These people need your leadership even more during these times. Your role is to coach this person, get the very best out of them and make them a satisfied, engaged and productive employee. Some employees get to this point a lot quicker than others.

In my career I was given corrective action at many different levels. I remember that once corrective action was given, it seemed I was an outcast, a problem child, and I now had to perform better than anyone else. When I used corrective action, I told my employees the same thing every time: "As far as I'm concerned, this issue is over. We understand each other, I have your assurance, and once this goes into my drawer, I will forget about it. If you cause me to go to that file with future poor performance, that is on you. Let's move forward from today." This always gave them a sense of relief and opportunity to begin anew.

TIME FOR FOLLOW-UP

This is often a forgotten part of the coaching session. It is vital for individual success that everyone involved gets back to the table and just does some follow-up. Is the plan working? Does it need to be tweaked? Is it helping Jim get back on track? Checking in with members of your team is something that needs to occur daily, but even more important, when there is coaching involved, this is something that cannot be missed. The power of follow-up cannot be overstated. It shows the importance of the situation, it shows you truly care, and it shows you're requiring accountability.

Another thing to note is that as the employee moves forward, changes behavior and reaches agreed-upon goals, they deserve a pat on the back. This positive reinforcement motivates, inspires and helps the individual grow. Positive reinforcement should happen soon after the accomplishment occurs. This will cement a positive influence with the employee. As time passes after the occurrence of the achievement, the reinforcement means less and has less influence.

These connections should also be face to face, or by call if necessary. A personal connection is what is needed here. It is vital the employee knows you care about them, they are important to you, and you show genuine interest in their professional development.

COACHING SOMETIMES FAILS

As leaders, sometimes we see potential in individuals before they see it in themselves. We strive to help them grow, develop and learn the skills so that when the time comes and they recognize their potential, they are ready for the next steps.

There were many individuals whose potential caught my eye, and I made it my mission to prepare them for greatness. I would sit them down, discuss what I saw in them and ask if they were interested in developing next-level skills. Sometimes this was met with excitement, other times a solid "not interested." Whatever the situation or reasons, you still try to help, keep an eye out for your employees' opportunities and guide them as necessary.

Remember, though, some people are just happy being who they are and will never step into the possibility of their potential.

Yes, this happens. I've known many people who had booming potential—you could just feel their energy; you knew that if you focused them, helped them grow, they could be an even more effective leader than you—but they were just truly happier in the life and position they were in. I remember thinking about a couple of such folks, *What a waste!*, or losing a little respect for them. This was a growth moment for me as a leader. In retrospect, it was not for me to pass judgment or think less of them because of the path they chose to take.

THE COACHED EMPLOYEE

So, let's say you sit down with an employee to address a work issue, and together you set goals for improvement and agree on how to proceed. What happens and how do you handle it if goals aren't reached and the agreement falls apart? Now coaching takes on a different focus. Instead of it being about the issue or problem, coaching now turns to the individual's accountability.

After the initial coaching session, you see the employee continue the same behavior. The best way to handle this situation is to follow these steps:

1. Once again bring the employee in for that face-to-face meeting and bring them back to the initial conversation.

2. Ask them to outline the intention of the last meeting and define their understanding of that meeting.

3. Once they outline their understanding, ask them if they believed a problem truly existed.

4. Then ask if they agreed to change their behavior based on the prior coaching session.

5. Ask if they made the agreed-upon changes.

6. When they say no, respond along the lines of, "It seems we have a bigger problem," or "Well, that's a problem too, then."

There are times employees need some time to prepare for something new. Remind them your professional relationship is based on trust, and if I say something to you as a leader, you know my word is true and I will follow up. This is true for the employee's word as well. Remind them that if you cannot trust their word, you can't have a professional relationship.

The rest of the conversation should continue like this:

1. Ask, "What happens to our working relationship if I cannot believe what you say?"

2. Guide them to the conclusion that if there is no trust, there will be no professional relationship.

3. Have them understand that if there is no basis for a professional relationship, your relationship will need to end. It is best if you can guide them to reach this conclusion themselves. You never want to say, "Do this, or I'll fire you." This will only put the employee on defense, and this is about being a coach, not a disciplinarian. You want them to understand that their behavior will result in them getting themselves fired.

4. Bring them back around to the original problem and have them share with you what that problem was and how they agreed to solve it.

5. Ask them when they agree to start solving the problem, so you know when to expect the change.

6. Be supportive and let them know you're glad they agreed to solve their problem.

7. End the discussion.

As the old saying goes, the proof of the pudding is in the eating. You will have to wait and see how things play out. Of course, if the employee again fails to make the changes they promised, it will be time to end your professional relationship with them. You may do this with the second or even third failure and subsequent discussion; it's up to you and how much slack you wish to give them. Our job is to coach and help employees be successful. Sometimes you just cannot do this within your organization, and when this occurs you should help them be successful somewhere else.

As a matter of formality, you should always document these discussions for your file. You never know when referring to them may come in handy.

Be a Coach

The workforce of today wants to be a part of an organization, not just a cog in a machine. For you to achieve your ultimate success as a leader, it is vital you show your workforce you value them, care about them and will do everything possible to help them become successful. The best way to do this is to become a master in coaching your workforce to success. This is a skill that will take years to develop, so start today and make this a foundation of your leadership toolbox.

When they know this, your workforce will not only appreciate you as a leader, but more important, they will follow you.

CHAPTER ELEVEN
My Favorite Leadership Quotes

A s the old saying goes, there is no need to reinvent the wheel. In business we are always looking for best practices to emulate in our organizations. When you develop a relationship with a mentor, it is their experience, reflection and wisdom they share with you. When it comes to leadership quotes, the bits of insight represented in this chapter pack an enormous amount of opportunity, hope and direction at your fingertips.

With each leadership quote, we receive mentorship from great, successful and progressive leaders. One favorite quote I use often comes from the Dalai Lama: "When you talk you are only repeating what you already know. But when you listen you may learn something new." As leaders who understand the importance of active listening, we know communication is a cornerstone of success. What the Dalai Lama shares in a couple of lines is that this is vital to learning and ultimately understanding.

In your leadership career, there will certainly be opportunities to overcome obstacles, mistakes and failures. Winston Churchill said, "Success is not final, failure is not fatal; it is the courage to continue that counts."

When you are stuck, looking for guidance or motivation/inspiration or trying to overcome an obstacle, do your homework and find quotes from leaders in that area that will guide you through. I often speak on using leadership quotes to guide your career; as you read the wisdom of successful leaders, take the time to reflect and determine what their quotes mean to you. If you find some you like, write them down and use them to guide your leadership style.

In this chapter I share some of my best leadership quotes—quotes from leaders and my friend and mentor John Maxwell. You will notice a couple of lines below each quote. Take time to reflect on what each quote means to you and jot down your thoughts about its meaning. I suggest using a pencil. As you grow in your leadership experience, the meaning you assign a certain quote may change.

CHRIS'S BEST LEADERSHIP QUOTES

"The difference between a good leader and a great leader is how they recover from failure."

_____

_____

_____

"It is not life, it is how you let life affect you."

_____

_____

_____

"Live your life, don't let your life live you."

_____

_____

_____

"If you want to be successful, get out of your own way."

"Whoever you think you are, that's who you become."

"Time is the enemy to your success; make today count."

"If you are a positional leader, you are in a great position to fail."

_____

_____

_____

"Unless you're a historian, stop thinking about yesterday."

_____

_____

_____

"Excuses lead to inactivity, inactivity leads to failure."

_____

_____

_____

"The longest distance between two points is a long way to reach your goal."

_____

_____

_____

"If your next big success were in your daily habits, you would have found it already."

_____

_____

_____

"You don't manage people, you manage processes. You lead, guide and coach people."

_____

_____

_____

"Leadership is both an art and a science. You must understand the science before you can paint the portrait of success."

_____

_____

_____

"A leader does not motivate people; a leader creates a safe environment so people can motivate themselves."

_____

_____

_____

"Don't be a leader who wishes something to happen. Be a leader who makes something happen."

_____

_____

_____

"There are two types of leaders: one who wishes, and one who wills."

_____

_____

_____

"The secret to success: What we value, we make time for. Value others."

_____

_____

_____

"Let persistence be the word that defines your character."

_____

_____

_____

"You only have two choices: Make progress or make excuses. Choose wisely."

_____

_____

_____

"Fear is just a story you like to tell yourself. Build a bridge toward positive thoughts."

_____

_____

_____

"Today is your day to create your tomorrow."

_____

_____

_____

"Accept all challenges. You can't pick the ones you like."

_____

_____

_____

"It's not the lack of time that's the problem. It's the lack of vision and direction that's the problem."

_____

_____

_____

"Every second is your chance to turn your life around."

_____

_____

_____

"Our scars are there to remind us that our past was real. These are the only thing we can truly call our own."

_____

_____

_____

"If you think it's expensive to hire a professional, wait till you hire an amateur."

_____

_____

_____

"You cannot change your past, but you can change your attitude about it."

_____

_____

_____

"We're not here to point fingers, we're here to fix problems."

_____

_____

_____

"Courage is all about kicking fear in its ass."

_____

_____

_____

"It's great to have a Plan B. Even in the military they gave me two parachutes."

_____

_____

_____

"If you find yourself telling people you're a leader, you're not."

_____

_____

_____

"Never allow your emotions to dictate your actions."

_____

_____

_____

"Don't waste time and energy on things you can't control."

_____

_____

_____

"Experience comes from mistakes, and mistakes comes from lack of experience."

"The true measure of leadership success is found in the satisfaction and engagement of the workforce."

"We cannot manage time; we can only manage our processes in allotted time."

"Stop hiring for the position and start hiring your future leaders."

"When you tell yourself you're going to try, you're giving yourself an excuse to fail."

MY CHOSEN QUOTES

"Set a goal so big you can't achieve it until you grow into the person who can."

—Zig Ziglar

_____

_____

_____

"The starting point of all achievement is desire."

—Napoleon Hill

_____

_____

_____

"Discipline is the bridge between goals and accomplishment."

—Jim Rohn

"Try not to become a man of success, but rather a man of value."

—Albert Einstein

"If opportunity doesn't knock, build a door."

—Milton Berle

_____

_____

_____

"The opportunist thinks of me and today, the statesmen think of us and tomorrow."

—Dwight D. Eisenhower

_____

_____

_____

"Faith in oneself is the best and safest course."

—Michelangelo

"Earn your leadership every day."

—Michael Jordan

"You can't build a reputation on what you're going to do."

—Henry Ford

"The time is always right to do the right thing."

—Martin Luther King, Jr.

"Every new day begins with possibilities. It is up to us to fill it with things that move us toward progress and peace."

—Ronald Reagan

_____

_____

_____

"Your smile is your logo, your personality is your business card, and the way you make others feel is your trademark."

—Zig Ziglar

_____

_____

_____

"The choice to have a great attitude is something that nobody or no circumstances can take from you."

—Zig Ziglar

"It always seems impossible till it's done."

—Nelson Mandela

"Ability is what you are capable of doing. Motivation determines what you do. Attitude determines how well you do it."

—Lou Holtz

_____

_____

_____

"Whatever your mind can conceive and believe, it can achieve."

—Napoleon Hill

_____

_____

_____

"Our greatest weakness is in giving up. The most certain way to succeed is to always try just one more time."

—Thomas Edison

_____

_____

_____

"When you talk, you are only repeating what you already know. But when you listen, you may learn something new."

—Dalai Lama

_____

_____

_____

"Too many of us are not living our dreams because we are living our fears."

—Les Brown

_____

_____

_____

"There are many ways of going forward, but only one way of standing still."

—Franklin D. Roosevelt

_____

_____

_____

"The task of a leader is to get their people from where they are to where they have never been."

—Henry Kissinger

"Do what you feel in your heart to be right, for you'll be criticized anyway."

—Eleanor Roosevelt

"Effective leadership is not about making speeches or being liked; leadership is defined by results, not attributes."

—Peter Drucker

_____

_____

_____

"Dear optimist, pessimist, and realist: While you guys were busy arguing about the glass of wine, I drank it! Sincerely, the opportunist!"

—Lori Greiner

_____

_____

_____

"The Wright brothers didn't have a pilot's license."

—Paul Martinelli

"Leadership is about making others better as a result of your presence and making sure that impact lasts in your absence."

—Sheryl Sandberg

"Don't let someone else's opinion of you become your reality."

—Les Brown

_____

_____

_____

"Talent wins games, but teamwork and intelligence wins championships."

—Michael Jordan

_____

_____

_____

"Our chief want is someone who will inspire us to be what we know we could be."

—Ralph Waldo Emerson

"The mediocre teacher tells. The good teacher explains. The superior teacher demonstrates. The great teacher inspires."

—William Arthur Ward

"If your actions inspire others to dream more, learn more, do more and become more, you are a leader."

—John Quincy Adams

"The greatest leader is not necessarily the one who does the greatest things. He is the one that gets the people to do the greatest things."

—Ronald Reagan

"Leadership is the capacity to transform vision into reality."

—Warren G. Bennis

"To lead people, walk beside them. As for the best leaders, the people do not notice their existence... When the best leader's work is done, the people say, 'We did it ourselves!'"

—Lao Tzu

---

*"The challenge of leadership is to be strong but not rude;
be kind but not weak; be bold but not bully; be thoughtful
but not lazy; be humble but not timid; be proud but not
arrogant; have humor but without folly."*

—Jim Rohn

_____

_____

_____

*"You do not lead by hitting people over the head. That's
assault, not leadership."*

—Dwight D. Eisenhower

_____

_____

_____

"Nearly all men can stand adversity, but if you want to test a man's character, give him power."

—Abraham Lincoln

"A man who wants to lead the orchestra must turn his back on the crowd."

—Max Lucado

"Optimism is the faith that leads to achievement."

—Helen Keller

_____

_____

_____

"The difference between successful people and others is how long they spend time feeling sorry for themselves."

—Barbara Corcoran

_____

_____

_____

Chris Cebollero

"Do not wait on a leader…look in the mirror, it's you!"

—Katherine Miracle

_____

_____

_____

"I don't go by the rule book. I lead from the heart, not the head."

—Diana Spencer

_____

_____

_____

JOHN MAXWELL QUOTES

One of my biggest professional honors has been becoming a member of the John Maxwell team. Having John as a mentor and, more important, as a friend has been amazing to my professional development. I have said this for many years now: Regardless of how much you think you know about leadership, when you sit in front of John Maxwell, you realize how much about leadership you do not know. If you are interested in learning more about joining the John Maxwell team, touch base, and I will introduce you to the right people.

John has some amazing experience, knowledge and great ways of connecting life, love and leadership. Enjoy some of my favorite John Maxwell quotes.

"The pessimist complains about the wind. The optimist expects it to change. The leader adjusts the sails."

_____

_____

_____

"To add value to others, one must first value others."

_____

_____

_____

"People may hear your words, but they feel your attitude."

_____

_____

_____

"People who use time wisely spend it on activities that advance their overall purpose in life."

_____

_____

_____

"As a leader, the first person I need to lead is me. The first person I should try to change is me."

_____

_____

_____

"Pride deafens us to the advice or warnings of those around us."

_____

_____

_____

"The best way a mentor can prepare another leader is to expose him or her to other great people."

_____

_____

_____

"The greatest mistake we make is living in constant fear that we will make one."

_____

_____

_____

"People buy into the leader before they buy into the vision."

_____

_____

_____

"The secret of your success is determined by your daily agenda."

_____

_____

_____

"Without failure, there is no achievement."

_____

_____

_____

"The measure of a leader is not the number of people who serve him but the number of people he serves."

_____

_____

_____

"A leader is great not because of his or her power, but because of his or her ability to empower others."

_____

_____

_____

"A great leader's courage to fulfill his vision comes from passion, not position."

_____

_____

_____

Chris Cebollero

"If we're growing, we're always going to be out of our comfort zone."

_____

_____

_____

"The challenge of leadership is to create change and facilitate growth."

_____

_____

_____

"There are no shortcuts to any place worth going."

_____

_____

_____

"Dreams don't work unless you do."

_____

_____

_____

"Leadership is evoking in others the capacity to dream."

_____

_____

_____

My Professional Network

I have a great professional network that encompasses thousands of professionals at different levels in their leadership journeys. One of the things I wanted to do was give my friends, peers and professional colleagues the opportunity to share their favorite leadership quotes. Some are original, others are borrowed from mentors or other great leaders.

"A leader does not tell, he shows! He is in the thick with his subordinates."

—Submitted by Erik Skoog

_____

_____

_____

"Respect is contagious."

—Submitted by Michael Cline

_____

_____

_____

"A strong nation, like a strong person, can afford to be gentle, firm, thoughtful and restrained. It can afford to extend a helping hand to others. It's a weak nation, like a weak person, that must behave with bluster and boasting and rashness and other signs of insecurity."

—Jimmy Carter, submitted by Stephanie Limmer

"When I am discussing an issue an employee refuses to address or acknowledge—or, worse, blames on one of my supervisors—I have a very simple quote. I'll use Jake as the supervisor:

"I can save you from Jake. I can save you from me. I cannot save you from yourself."

—Submitted by Neil White

"Ten percent of your workforce is great, and they are the reason you come to work. Ten percent are terrible and take up most of your time. The other 80% are watching how you deal with the other two groups before deciding which side of the fence they are going to fall on."

—Jack Stout, submitted by Dave Gammell

"Your wholeness is based upon your awareness of your brokenness."

—Submitted by Eric Chase

"Trust but verify."

—Ronald Reagan, submitted by Sarah McEntee

_____

_____

_____

"There is a lot of theater in EMS. Teach your field EMS employees, 'If you can treat the patient, treat the crowd.'"

—Submitted by Janet Smith

_____

_____

_____

"What we have done for ourselves alone dies with us; what we have done for others is immortal."

—Albert Pike, submitted by Jay Cebollero

"Lead, follow or get the hell out of my way."

—George S. Patton, Jr., submitted by Randy Ingram

"Grit is the extra effort you do after you get tired of doing the extra effort you already did."

—Submitted by Kris Kaull

_____

_____

_____

"I've learned that people will forget what you said, people will forget what you did, but people will never forget how you made them feel."

—Maya Angelou, submitted by Jennifer Cordia

_____

_____

_____

"When you're ready, the comeback is always better and stronger then the setback."

—Submitted by Debbie Self

"Leadership is influence, doing the right things and showing the way. But at its essence, true leadership is not dependent on position. It is what moves us forward and improves the lives of others."

—Submitted by David A. Miles, PhD

"Leadership is not a position, it's an attitude and a character of strength."

—Submitted by Anna Sarnacka-Smith

_____

_____

_____

"Leaders build other leaders, not followers."

—Submitted by Jamie Davis

_____

_____

_____

"Treat people like people and adults like adults."

—Submitted by Chris Robinson

_____

_____

_____

"When you come into an established organization as a new leader, it's best to drop the illusion that you're the boss. Instead figure out where they are heading and run alongside until they see you've caught up. Ask permission to join. Then you can engage in a conversation about what you might have to contribute."

—Submitted by Mike Taigman

_____

_____

_____

"It's not that you can't, it's that you won't."

—Submitted by Chris Robinson

"A good leader takes a little more than his share of the blame and a little less than his share of the credit."

—John Maxwell, submitted by Jennifer Dones

I am sure that in reading this chapter, you may have thought of a quote from your mentor or some of your own leadership quotes. Write them below and begin developing your own wisdom. As you write your own quotes, share them with me and my network on my Facebook page, www.facebook.com/cebolleroassociates. I look forward to hearing from you!

_____

_____

_____

_____

_____

_____

_____

_____

_____

_____

_____

Conclusion

Why did you decide to become a leader? Was it for the increase in salary? The parking spot? Maybe the status? If you had self-serving reasons for taking the position you're in, there is very little chance of you being successful.

But if you became a leader because you thought you could make a difference for the people you serve, then allow the skills in this book guide you to your ultimate success. Just like any other science, when you use the science of leadership, beautiful things happen within your departments and organizations.

Success does not happen by chance; there is no genie in a bottle you can rub and wish for leadership success. I know—I looked for this bottle earlier in my career and failed with every grain of sand that slipped through my fingers. It was not until I learned that practicing the skills of leadership truly made the difference.

Follow the lessons in this book, and I promise you, you too will become an ultimate success.

On a final note, if I can be a resource in any way, if you are looking for a coach or need some organizational development or process improvement, please reach out to me at chris@chriscebollero.com.

Please consider leaving a review of this book on Amazon to assist the readers coming behind you.

Cheers!

About the Author

Chris Cebollero is an internationally recognized leadership specialist, best-selling author, coach and motivational lecturer. His dynamic and energetic speaking style has entertained, motivated and educated individuals, groups and teams for more than three decades. Chris is currently the senior partner of his own consulting firm specializing in leadership development, individual and executive coaching, and organizational process improvement. Chris has been seen on ABC, NBC, CBS and Fox. He is a certified member of the John Maxwell team and an official member of the Forbes Coaching Council. Chris has spent 30 years in the emergency medical services career field and continues to be an advocate for delivering the best care possible.

Chris is available for one-on-one or group coaching, organizational leadership development and training, and organizational growth and development. If you want to book Chris to speak at your event, contact him via e-mail at chris@chriscebollero.com or call (314) 297-6850.

Join Chris as he hosts the Ultimate Leadership podcast. You can join the discussion at http://ultimateleadership.blubrry.com.

Check out Chris's best-selling book *Ultimate Leadership: 10 Rules for Success* on Amazon.

FOR MORE INFORMATION

For more information or to contact Chris, visit his social media pages:

Facebook—www.facebook.com/cebolleroassociates/

Twitter—@ChiefofEMS

LinkedIn—www.linkedin.com/in/ chris-cebollero-leadership-consultant-2940bb33

Online—http://www.chriscebollero.com

Notes

Chris Cebollero

Chris Cebollero

www.ingramcontent.com/pod-product-compliance
Lightning Source LLC
Chambersburg PA
CBHW071428170526
45165CB00001B/436